MOURNING MODERNISM

Mourning Modernism

LITERATURE, CATASTROPHE, AND THE POLITICS OF CONSOLATION

LECIA ROSENTHAL

FORDHAM UNIVERSITY PRESS

New York 2011

Copyright © 2011 Fordham University Press

Fordham University Press has no responsibility for the
persistence or accuracy of URLs for external or third-party
Internet websites referred to in this publication and does not
guarantee that any content on such websites is, or will
remain, accurate or appropriate.

Fordham University Press also publishes its books in a
variety of electronic formats. Some content that appears in
print may not be available in electronic books.

Library of Congress Cataloging-in-Publication Data is
available from the publisher.

Printed in the United States of America
13 12 11   5 4 3 2 1
First edition

CONTENTS

FIGURES

ACKNOWLEDGMENTS

I acknowledge the support of Tufts University, where a Junior Faculty Research Grant and a Mellon Faculty Research Fellowship helped make this book possible. I am also grateful to colleagues in the Department of English who stood with me in solidarity along the way. In particular, I thank Lee Edelman for his consistent support. I also thank Linda Bamber, Jay Cantor, Radiclani Clytus, Kevin Dunn, Sheila Emerson, Carol Flynn, John Fyler, Rebecca Gibson, Judith Haber, Joe Litvak, Jonathan Strong, Ichiro Takayoshi, Michael Ullman, and Jonathan Wilson. To Virginia Jackson, who kept the conversation going and invited me to see a more expansive view of intellectual and institutional life, I am tremendously grateful. To my students, without whose voices I would not have been able to think, I acknowledge a debt all the more inexhaustible for not being able to list them by name.

Many colleagues and friends have contributed in substantial but im-measurable ways to this project. Docsan Levine and Karin Stephan changed my mind when I thought it least possible. I thank Stathis Gour-gouris, Martin Harries, Joseph Massad, and Gayatri Chakravorty Spivak for reading my work and providing venues in which to share it with others. I am grateful to Shakeel Bhatti, Jennifer Gerson, Moeen Lashari, Andrew Rubin, Michael Rubinoff, Ryan Shiraki, Amy Toothman, Lale Uner, Mi-chel Vernes, and Jonathan Zittrain for their encouragement and for years of brilliant friendship, and to Diana Reese, my constant collaborator, for keeping faith with the inconsolable and for the beauty of her words. I am indebted to Jonathan Lutes, whose generosity has always been so inspir-ing, for responding without hesitation to my request to translate Benja-min's radio addresses. Enormous thanks to Helen Tartar, as well as to Eric Newman, Teresa Jesionowski, and the readers at Fordham University Press. For his patience and kindness, and for everything, I thank Chris Coletta, to whom I dedicate this book.

MOURNING MODERNISM

Introduction

This book focuses on the writing of finitude and catastrophe in the twenti-eth century, taking as its point of departure the oft-repeated, epochalizing characterization of the century as a turning point in the history of violence and destruction, or the pivotal yet ambivalent claim that for the first time in the history of the world, humanity has the power to bring about the end of human life, to annihilate the human as species and ideal. If it "was during the last century that humanity became capable of destroying itself, whether directly through nuclear war or indirectly through the alteration of the conditions necessary for survival,"[1] supposing such a newly attained capa-bility for autodestruction to be already under way, how are we to locate, think, and call on the humanity presumed responsible and said to have put itself at risk? How to represent, anticipate, mourn the fictive collectivity of (posthumous, remainderless, futureless) humanity? Literary criticism, and so-called nuclear criticism in particular, has taken up the fantasy of such an unprecedented, all-encompassing, and remainderless end, and the prob-lems it raises for thinking the last and unsurvivable event, the event that would break with all thought and any writing of the event. Maurice Blan-chot and Jacques Derrida, among others, have questioned the launching rhetoric of the "new" apocalypse, along with its privative constitution of collective belonging, of a humanity joined in the spectacular threat of a shared, unsurvivable autodemise. *Mourning Modernism* draws on such criticism to forge connections between modernism's drive for an aesthetics of the new and the utopian longing for catastrophe's end.

Much attention has been given to the representation of individual death in modernist poetics, and therein to formal, psychoanalytic, and feminist concerns regarding the prose of elegy, the critique of melancholia, and the difficult language and temporality of trauma. Similarly, modernist criticism has taken up the burdens of mass death and the aesthetics of total war (particularly in relationship to the legacies of the First World War) as they inform the narrative and history of modernism. *Mourning Modernism* critiques and suspends the periodizing frame that limits modernism to the period before the Second World War, taking its cue from debates about the postmodern (and in particular about Lyotard's focus on the postmodern and the sublime), debates that can be understood most effectively through a rethinking of modernism's ambivalent investment in totality, including that "negative" presentation of totality associated with the sublime.

As an aesthetics of overload, terror, and the threat of the breaking point, the sublime represents a prehistory for understanding contemporary debates on trauma. Without reducing one to the other (for the differences between and within each are many), one might trace the genealogical lines that traverse the two categories. The sublime posits a mixed investment in pain and pleasure, violence and survival, a mediated experience of terror imposed and lived through. Trauma articulates the event of pain and its (failure to) register, calling attention to the problematic status of an event that takes place by not taking place, or that only and always takes place in delay of its proper place. In addition to carrying resonances of violence, the aesthetics of sublimity and the writing of trauma share attachments to suffering privations immeasurable, or to experiences that, in their compulsions of force and powers of overwhelming magnitude, threaten to undermine not only the subject's psychic integrity or physical survival but also the ability to *think*—to anticipate, recollect, and symbolize—the very experience of the (nearly) annihilating encounter.

Trauma's unhousing of experience meets with sublimity at the crucial point where contemporary culture, with its multiplication of compensatory pleasures and virtual prophylaxes, demands a reading of the concomitant insistence on the real—a compulsive desire to reopen and bleed the wound, to deepen the sustaining cut, to experience again and anew a fantasy of the raw edges of splitting, breaking, and disfiguration. The vacillating desire for risk taking and danger aversion returns to the rhetoric of modernity's variations on malaise: From the dull pulsations of disenchant-ment to the normalized bourgeois pathologies of boredom, paralysis, and enfeeblement, the sublime offers to compel, and the traumatic event insists on threatening to impose and withhold, a counterforce to the draining, seemingly fixed forms of regulative normativity and its holding patterns, the unending lament of *taedium vitae*. It is with rather than against the strangling sense of being stuck, as if inured to the standardization of dan-gers and calmatives alike, that the late sublime, like the mixed attachments of trauma, finds its launching rhetoric and vital concerns.

Late modernism, rather than a historically determined and finite period (say, a designation for the interwar years as they approach the retrospec-tively asserted "end" of modernism), composes an aesthetics of lateness that probes the very question of modernism's *terminality*, or the writing of finitude within modernism's drive for the new. If the notion of "late life" strikes associations with dusk and death, nearing-to-end and posthumous, symbolic forms of survival (the iterative returns of memory, mourning, melancholia; the symbolic afterlives summoned through memorialization of the name; the unwanted apparitions of the ghost or the violent undead), the late aesthetic similarly evokes and resists a temporality of limited ex-tension and naturalized organicity. As in the rhetoric of decadence and its tropes of decline (from the overripe turned rotten to the life-form that refuses to die), the late aesthetic suggests not only a narrative of nearing-to-term but also the excesses of aberrant superannuation, the monstrous overgrowth that insists on persisting beyond term. The late aesthetic, dis-placing organic life and natural death as a substratum for the thinking of finitude, asserts an ambivalent, untimely belatedness, a sense of coming "after" that does not presuppose continuity of transition or successive in-heritance. In modernism's aesthetics of departure, the problem of the past imposes the weight of an unassimilated, ever-burgeoning dispersal of loss. Both proleptic and retrospective, anticipatory and backward-looking, late-ness is at odds with the neat distinctions between the (first) "now" of the event and the (secondary) "now" of posterity.

Chapter 1, "Catastrophe Culture, Atrocity Supplements," investigates the category of catastrophe as it emerges alongside modernism's tropes of the "new" and the "unprecedented" to assert, often with a sense of unprecedented urgency, unresolved tensions within modernity. Amid mo-dernity's temporality of acceleration and the "annihilation of space by time,"[2] the possibility of global catastrophe emerges as a threat to every remaining boundary (indexes of difference, including those of the eco-nomic, cultural, national, ecological, biological, and religious). At the same time, catastrophe erupts to render visible the ongoing contradictions within capitalism and its commensurating logics of systematization, homogenization, and exchange. At the margins of such systems, catastrophe designates something other to, something more than, the negative moment of an inevitable dialectic of progress and containment. Like the death drive, catastrophe points to a beyond that can never be placed either inside or outside a prior logic of integration, meaning, or futurity.

Returning again and again to the scene of the end—the end of the world, the end of history, the end of the future—catastrophe culture draws on and draws out the fantasy of protective immunity, a prolongation of the paradoxical structure that takes pleasure in longing for always yet more: for more of the same, for more than more of the same. In the logic of the repetition compulsion, the allure of catastrophe returns to a paradoxical refrain that writes "for the future," articulating a desire for no more (no more war, no more poverty, no more death), a privative ideal whose counterpart is a fantasy of mastery and containment, a fantasy of controlled mastery of the future, a fantasy for the future to be, ideally and impossibly, no more than the end of futurity. The refrain that seeks to neutralize the "more" of the future as more of the same finds its apotheosis in the century's oft-made observation that, with the launch of new forms of viral velocity and the potentially irreversible effects of new technologies of splicing and their unpredictable vectors of spanning (from the lethal fallout of the atom bomb to the spread of genetically modified organisms), the century inaugurates, for the first time in history, the threat of a man-made, secular apocalypse: the end of the world but without revelation, the remainderless and last event, the extinction of man-as-species.

The threat of the "end of the world" takes various forms: the end of humanity, the end of nature, the exhaustion of the earth as habitat. The related concerns of world-ending—the representation of a single, all-encompassing world and the projection of a world at its end—find their initial nodal point in the emergent discourse of spatial finitude: the figure of the shrinking earth. As the globe is increasingly traversed by technologies of connectivity and communication, and as it becomes possible to think of the world as *one*, the limits of expansion introduce a rhetoric of scarcity and subtraction: no more undiscovered space, no more room to expand, no more territory left to conquer. By the late nineteenth century, what was once an end to be attained—the cartographic saturation of the globe by empire, industry, technology—became a limit to be displaced and deferred. If, as some have argued, the imperial project of territorial mapping induced a shift in the thinking and location of utopia, a dislocation from space to time,[3] modernism responded by co-opting the claims of perfectibility and questioning the utopian extension of progress.

Read through the marxian critique of the category and narrative of originary ("primitive") accumulation, or the argument that capital continually recodes the location and lines of its substrate, inventing the taxonomy of nature, prehistory, and untouched remainder not once but over and over again, the refrain of "shrinking earth" articulates a signature tension in the twentieth century's schizoid logic of finitude and catastrophe. The writing of the last of extimate earth and the fantasy of the end of distance are, like the event of originary accumulation, iterative in their lines of exhaustion and their annexations of the final frontier. Incorporating and relocating the limit, late capitalism normalizes the competing narratives of scarcity and survival. With the biopolitical regularization of the mass, or the management of "man-as-species" (Foucault), the threat of the ultimate end—the event as superhistorical catastrophe, violence of unthinkable partition, breach and breakdown in excess of every norm—becomes, in its own right, a fetish, covering and standing in for the (missing) radical break, the revolutionary turn that would cut into bourgeois culture and its normalizing forces. Within modernism, the desire for the radical break, or the surge of the quickening rupture and the encounter with the beyond or alterity of death, appears in the aesthetics of shock (notably in Baudelaire and Benjamin), as well as in the transvaluation of violence in the aesthetics of total war.

The modernist writing of catastrophe, I argue, affirms, with great ambivalence, the power of the aesthetic by staging the imagination at the brink of destruction. Even as such a confrontation evokes the tradition of the sublime and the long-standing poetics of the "sublime turn," the modernist return to the sublime comes with its own propulsion-in-danger. The force of the modernist sublime emerges as an aesthetics of the world at war. Reading Kant's elaboration of the war sublime alongside the anticipatory finality in the rhetoric of a "war to end all war," I situate the emergence of modernism within the competing discourses of violence and the end of violence, fragmentation and privative totality, individual death and species survival.

Chapter 2, "Virginia Woolf: Reading Remains," focuses on the relationship between modernism and the First World War. I read modernism's aesthetic desire, that is to say its elevation of the new over the known, the experiment over tradition, as embedded within the related forces of catastrophe and mass culture, war and capitalism, destruction and inertia. As much as modernism may want to move forward, toward an uncharted space and autarchic form of writing, it never escapes the anxiety that drives the search: The fear that the space of the new, the significant allure of the cutting edge, has been overtaken and exhausted, saturated by the accumulated residue of so many nonalternatives. The museum and the market are exposed as compromise formations; so too the legacies of Romanticism and its critics (from the notion of aesthetic autonomy to the embrace of insignificance) are inherited as damaged goods. I trace these concerns about belatedness and the threats of exhaustion as they contribute to early science fiction and utopias of the antiurban, postdisaster pastoral. In the emergent discourse of aerial warfare, such texts anticipate the rhetoric of the "war to end all wars." Together with such concerns, I read the modernism of Virginia Woolf's postwar (or "interwar") novel, *To the Lighthouse*.

In Chapter 3, "Walter Benjamin on Radio: Catastrophe for Children," I turn to Benjamin's writings on new media. Although much attention has been given to his work on photography, the extant manuscripts of Benjamin's radio addresses have been overlooked. This chapter reads two radio broadcasts for children written and delivered by Benjamin on German radio in February and March 1932. In "The Railway Disaster at the Firth of Tay," the story of a train wreck is ostensibly put to use to describe an early moment in a history of technological progress, a history that has, Benjamin reassures his audience, finally achieved a victory over technological failure and the large-scale catastrophes that end in significant loss of life. In "The Mississippi Flood, 1927," Benjamin similarly presents a tragedy in the form of fairy tale, in this case a narrative of a natural catastrophe within its political context. In both stories, Benjamin uses the relatively new medium of radio in a playful, and at the same time entirely serious, attempt to transmit a barely encoded warning. As if history were in the hands of children, he appeals to them to interrupt the repetition compulsion that is already signaling the disaster of Germany's political future. Fanciful and desperate, these texts, like those by Verne and Grandville that fascinated Benjamin throughout his career, are forms of science fiction.

Chapter 4, "On the Late Sublime: W. G. Sebald's *The Rings of Saturn*," brings together in the figure of Sebald the Anglo-German trajectory of the preceding discussions. Sebald's recent rise to critical prominence can be attributed to the ongoing, and still unresolved, debates over Holocaust memory and the legacies of the Second World War. Focusing on Sebald's novel *The Rings of Saturn: An English Pilgrimage*, I read a contemporary aesthetics of exhaustion and subtraction, an insistent itinerancy that takes distance only through withdrawal. Sebald's work borrows heavily on and tacitly invokes some of the legacies of the twentieth-century avant-garde. His use of a mixed-media aesthetics that combines prose with photographic image and found object recalls the practices of Dada and of minimalism but with none of the playfulness and errant intensity of the former and without the latter's strictness of the intentionless work. Still, in combining the gestures of montage and collage, Sebald creates an aesthetics remarkable for its apparent evenness of affect and its narrator's seeming lack of desire. In my reading of Sebald's novel, I focus first on an acute tension between the intensity of debate surrounding the representation of Holocaust memory in Sebald's work, on the one hand, and the text's own lack of interest in issues of veracity in its allusion to the camps, on the other. With the strange and uprooting citational style that has become a signature of Sebald's work, *The Rings of Saturn* reproduces, without attribution and with no mention of his name in the text, an image taken by the British photographer George Rodger at Bergen-Belsen in April 1945. The novel's suspension of the image's history has gone unnoticed in the criticism, a lacuna that is all the more interesting for the status of the photographer's work in the related narratives of the history of photography and the Holocaust in the archive. I argue that Sebald stretches the paradoxes of the late sublime to their maximum, postarchival pitch, taking us beyond what many critics, following the work of Marianne Hirsch, have called the generations of "postmemory." I then situate Sebald within wider debates on modernism and postmodernism to suggest that the latter bears the costs of modernism's failure.

CHAPTER I

Catastrophe Culture, Atrocity Supplements

But . . . for you, no wound.

ROLAND BARTHES, *Camera Lucida*

In its edition of April 28, 1945, *The Illustrated London News* published a "four-page detachable supplement." The additional pages came with small print: "N.B.—This four-page detachable supplement contains photographic evidence of the sadistic brutalities practiced by the Germans at various internment camps now in Allied hands. These revelations of coldly-calculated massacre and torture are given as a record for all time of German crimes, and are intended for our adult readers only. Our subscribers with young families whom they would not desire to see the photographs, can remove these pages, which are easily detachable, by a sharp pull, from the remainder of our issue."[1] Anticipating the risk of unwanted exposure, the paper builds in a structure for maintaining remove, protection through the cut of detachment. Prophylaxis of the sharp pull, advance warning of a danger.

In the atrocity supplement, the newspaper tries to appease, and thus puts on display, its doubt over the justification for exhibiting the images: over whether and how they should be shown, and to whom; over whether and how they can be shown without offending an unstated yet implied standard of public morality and aesthetic judgment; over an expectation of an offense to the limits of taste and reason, an offense whose ostensible victim, in the figure of the child, widens to include the unprepared, naive reader, the unguided or insufficiently prepared reader for whom "happening upon" such images, as if by chance, would be too much, even devastating, an unassimilable shock, a form of secondary trauma. Susan Sontag's frequently cited narration of her own early encounter with just such images (they have, she suggests, become altogether too much of a type) places emphasis on novelty as the condition of their force, a kind of primal scene in which the representation of suffering, in the object of the photograph, may indeed become a fetish. "Photographs shock insofar as they show something novel. Unfortunately, the ante keeps getting raised—partly through the proliferation of such images of horror. One's first encounter with the photographic inventory of ultimate horror is a kind of revelation, the prototypically modern revelation: a negative epiphany. For me, it was photographs of Bergen-Belsen and Dachau which I came across by chance in a bookstore in Santa Monica in July 1945."[2] Contingent on a certain naïveté and newness, located in the historical moment when "such" photographs (if of a kind they are) had not yet become so widespread and normalized, the wound occasioned by Sontag's first encounter has, she suggests, ceded to a world of nonstop exhibitions of atrocity, an anesthetizing and corrupting proliferation. "Once one has seen such images, one has started down the road of seeing more—and more. Images transfix. Images anesthetize."[3]

Engaging the rhetoric and temporality of such anesthetizing repetition (the effects of cumulative resistance that Sontag redoubles in her troping of addition: "more—and more"), *Mourning Modernism: Literature, Catastrophe, and the Politics of Consolation* is an inquiry into the shutdown that does not cease to disturb, indeed that only continues to compel and insist evermore—returning us to the demand for an addition in surplus, to the insistence on an ethics and aesthetics that would give, to the viewer, critic, and perhaps the world at large, something more than ever before: a demand for more truth, for more than truth, for a form of representation somehow sufficiently self-critical of all preceding demands for and presentations of ostensibly new forms of truth. From the failures of the aesthetic, both with and against the history of modernism, to have curtailed or redeemed the century's many, indeed some would say countless, repetitions of atrocities unprecedented, to the ongoing demand that the aesthetic justify itself in the face of mass death and suffering (or, alternatively, in the impossibility or absence of any face-to-face immediacy or ethics of encounter), the compulsion for more takes shape not only in the claims of evidence but also in the demand to supplement the overflow of atrocity with an affirmative spin.

*   *   *

The metaphoric catastrophe is precisely that, the failure of any anchor.

Catherine Malabou, *Counterpath*

Whereas the atrocity supplement makes itself both indispensable for the full revelation of the truth and disposable for the protection of the not-yet-adult (it is "easily detachable"), in Sontag's world, such images of "ultimate horror" no longer have the power to disclose any positive or newly revealed truth. Merely the repetition of a once revelatory but now stalled "negative epiphany," their only truth-function, it would seem, is to reinforce the image in its already established lack of effect, a moribund negativity. Nor, according to Sontag, would such images require the additional shield of supplementary detachment. Rather than the effect of protection through controlled nonexposure, detachment has become a widespread condition, the cumulative saturation effected by a history of overexposure. In the logic of Sontag's proposition, the danger posited by the atrocity supplement shifts: From the threat of a viewer's encounter as shock, the risk has become an image that can never be shocking enough.

Shocking enough—but for what? Sontag's argument follows the tension of the supplement, which, as Derrida has shown, works through the double movement of being both merely additive (it fits into or confirms an already established order) and super- or overadditive (if the already established order is, supposedly on its own, fully constituted, what need or room for more?), both "easily detachable" and altogether dangerous.[4] In Sontag's narrative, the supplement becomes an issue of resistance to *and* desire for more of the image: Images of atrocity, with their power to transfix, compel through a power of sheer fascination, a form of compulsive attraction (perhaps one of the century's many pathologies of addiction, the attachment with diminishing returns), which, in repetition of the experience of dissatisfaction, eventually neutralizes the force of encounter, canceling the shock effects of the image. No longer the medium of a frightful but possibly instructive and even ethical encounter, the photograph of ultimate horror now transmits only the negative returns of the banal and the same: the same predictable negativity, the image in its lack of (proper) effect, the narcissistic dead end of an anesthetized, benumbed, impotent viewer.

Sontag's argument exposes the desire, that of the critic and perhaps of the viewer as well, for the image to continue to deliver always yet more:

The representation of atrocity, particularly that of the worst of privations (atrocity is always an issue of cruelty and violence), should, at all costs, signify, introduce, and deliver an effective and definitive gain. The ongoing, anxious demand for "more—and more" reiterates a structure of supplementarity in which the dividends of "more" are divided between repetition and deferral, return and rupture (hence the doubled extenuation of Sontag's phrasing: "more—and more"). The desire for additional, supplementary spoils attendant on the representation of atrocity follows the paradoxical structure of the repetition compulsion: in the desire for more, a return to the same; in the insistence on more of the same, a prolongation and deferral of the desire for even and still yet *more*: more of more-as-the-same, yet also something else again, perhaps even, if such is still possible, something altogether new. Here, in the movement between a drive for "more" that would seek to restore the priority of a past and its established disorders (whether coded as pathological or normative, or in some other order of truth, say that of a "return" to the order and truth of the properly Kantian sublime)[5] and a drive for "more" that would, even in reiterating the appeal of such an established priority, nonetheless lend interest and room for an opening, something like a space for a critical turn—in the movement between these two forms of the insistence on "more" lies, perhaps, more than a reading of one critic's desire. Rather, at stake is a wider rhetoric, increasingly in circulation within the last century, that questions and seeks to justify the dissemination of terror's image, an aesthetics of atrocity.

The demand for a necessary but uncertain surplus—more meaning, more justification, more advantage of return—asserts itself in more than one rhetoric or ideology of judgment. There is, for instance, the repeated demand that requires, at a minimum, that the substitutive experience of atrocity differentiate its appeal from the lowly allure of the merely pornographic, that base economy of the libidinal whose "obscene" pleasures, always lurking below the line of the socially acceptable, offend all the more for calling attention to the instability of the (moral, aesthetic) law, to the arbitrary coding of morality, and the uncertain grounds for issuing aesthetic judgment. (Thus for Sontag, pornography and evil, and by extension aesthetics and ethics, are inextricably linked—through what she calls a "law.")[6] Yet the anxiety over distinguishing a "proper" versus an "improper" use of the image extends beyond the ongoing debates over pornography. And, notwithstanding the specificity of the atrocity supplement and its focus on the *photographic* image as medium and object, concerns over such paired terms as representation and atrocity, aesthetics and suffering, art and horror, writing and disaster, narrative and trauma are not limited to photography. The last century saw the proliferation and intermixing of new media, technologies, and forms of representation, an accumulation of more and more images to archive, sell, and redistribute. Death was said to disappear (the argument of, among others, the French historian Philippe Ariès),[7] and, at the same time, genocide and mass death were industrialized. In the context of such developments, anesthetization notwithstanding, mass culture remains fascinated with consuming scenes of "unimaginable" horror. For Walter Benjamin, such fascination represents an expression of a fundamental antinomy: At the limit of the claims of experience, modern warfare and the escalation of the means of destruction occasion a (mal)-adaptive, shock-absorbing, commodity aesthetics, the fetish for death, the projection of species annihilation on screen. "Its [mankind's] self-alienation has reached such a degree that it can experience its own destruction as an aesthetic pleasure of the first order."[8]

The refrain of the demand of "more" from the artifact, the document, and the image—the insistence that they should add to a greater good; that they should contribute more rather than less to some higher, perhaps as yet unrecognized or insufficiently acknowledged, insight—is a persistent, if also differentiated and inconsistently framed, demand of twentieth-century culture and criticism. With the accumulated losses of atrocity (itself an aporia: how to inscribe the "loss of loss," or how to mark loss without merely "filling in" the void with more and more indexes of accumulated information, projects of archivization, the accumulation of the object as memento mori), the already difficult relationships between history and narrative, event and representation face new and additional demands (another question of the supplement). Such demands place pressure on the act and experience of representation to make "good" the encounter with loss, to imbue the representation of historical atrocity with some form of gain: perhaps with a new truth or form of insight; perhaps, to the contrary, with a reiteration of the authority, meaning, and resonance of older, previously established narratives; perhaps with an insistence on the need to elevate, honor, reclaim humanist values, or, for that matter, an antihumanist critique of such values. They may also articulate, alongside the imposing desire for an aesthetics of redemption, reparation, or transcendence, a resistance to such pressure, an internal critique of the driving desire for supplementing (or even overcoming or sublimating altogether) aesthetic pleasure with moral meaning, aesthetic experience with a definitive insight and revelatory end.[9]

It would be naive, therefore, to suggest that the related critiques of anesthetic resistance (lack of affect) and commodity culture's circulation of the image for mere consumption or "atrocity tourism" (implying, perhaps, too much pleasure, the wrong kind of pleasure, or simply mindless enjoyment), insofar as they return to the desire for "more" from the aesthetic experience or the work of art, do so in a vacuum, as if they were not also implicated in the historical problematic from which such a desire would emerge.[10] It is just this ongoing, unresolved dialectic—the movement between, on the one hand, a critique of the historical failures and limitations of the aesthetic, and, on the other, a critique of that critique, an engagement with the limits of any proposed or ostensible resolution to the historical, formal, and political problems haunting the aesthetic—that Theodor Adorno insists on in his return to the problem of "art after Auschwitz." Despite being associated with the apparent definitiveness of the aesthetic ban suggested in his phrase, "It is barbaric to continue to write poetry after Auschwitz," Adorno, perhaps more than anyone, has insisted on problematizing any solution to the aesthetic at its limits or the fulfillment of any political program or theory that would claim to have realized the proper definition, sphere, and indeed limits of art.[11] If, as Adorno argues, no work succeeds in negating the reality from which it nonetheless and necessarily escapes (Adorno, like Blanchot, will insist on allowing for the incommensurable distance between the work and the world from which it emerges, a world in which it nonetheless remains a part: "There is no content, no formal category of the literary work that does not, however transformed and however unawarely, derive from the empirical reality from which it has escaped"), similarly, the demand for "more" from the work, including the critical demand that the work of art partake of a redemptive elevation, as a negation of a culture of anesthesia, despair, or cynicism, can hardly claim to start from a zero point of history or to derive its priorities from a pure metaphysics of value. Even if one wants to agree that ours is a culture dominated by anesthesia and amnesia, it is also true that there is simply no laying to rest the scars of violence and the ghosts of past suffering.

*   *   *

But for pain words are lacking.

Virginia Woolf, *The Waves*

"Down the road of seeing more—and more," as Sontag's phrasing would have it, are several interrelated forms of the demand for "more," perhaps foremost among them the necessary supplement of the ethical

demand, the "more" of quality, meaning, and value that would differentiate and justify an aesthetics of horror, the art of shock. Such a demand
puts pressure on the representation and substitutive experience of suffering, calling into question the ideological function of and the nature of
pleasure (and pain) derived from art "after Auschwitz." Adorno's remarks, along with his many elaborations of the problem in other contexts,
present only one (albeit perhaps the most widely debated) launching
point for a discussion of the aesthetic at its limits, in this case a form of a
representational ban. As the century goes on, the taboo against art in the
wake of the Holocaust plays a pivotal role in aesthetic, literary, psychoanalytic, and cultural theory as the specter of the unrepresesentable returns
to insist on and yet problematize the language and claims of the limit-
event: how to speak of events of terror, violence, and desubjectification
that, having deprived their victims of the capacity to represent or testify
in their own language and for their "own" experience (the extent of privation troubles the very idea of "own-ness," or what is considered proper
to the subject), threaten to remain unspoken? At stake is not only the
critique of an overly accommodating, conciliatory, or compensatory aesthetic (which would simply skip over such problems), but also questions
about the very limits of representation and the problem of imagining the
"unimaginable."

"N'invoquons pas l'inimaginable," writes Georges Didi-Huberman, a
paradoxical rejoinder and imperative all the more interesting for its obvious performative contradiction: Let us not invoke the unimaginable.[12]
This critique follows on a critical history that, for varying reasons, resisted
the notion that it was possible, whether through sympathetic identification
or comparison to precedent, to imagine the extreme and unprecedented
experience of the camps. Thus, Hannah Arendt, who is perhaps more
widely known for putting into circulation the phrase the "banality of evil,"
the punctuating moment of her critique of the discourse for which the
perpetrators of genocide remain beyond understanding and exceptional to
the dictates of reason, argues in another context, "There are no parallels
to the life in the concentration camps. Its horror can never be fully em-
braced by the imagination for the very reason that it stands outside of life
and death. It can never be fully reported for the very reason that the survivor returns to the world of the living, which makes it impossible for him
to believe fully in his own past experiences."[13]

The rhetorical negotiation with the category of the "unimaginable"
inevitably intersects with, if unintentionally, obliquely, and perhaps

against claims to better judgment, the rhetoric and tradition of the sublime. The unimaginable suggests an aesthetics of incompletion and resistance: The spectacle of unprecedented atrocity introduces but cannot fully comprehend, explain, account for, or make sense of the specter of suffering and terror in excess of all reason and normative bounds. The unprecedented—a category and threshold to be explored further below—suggests an event without place, an event whose like has never before taken place, and moreover an event that will challenge whatever terms may already be in place for thinking, symbolizing, and grasping the horrifying magnitude and nature of the atrocity.[14]

As nearly every theory of the sublime has argued, the threat of the unimaginable, often contingent upon an overwhelming, unsynthesizable sensory experience or an encounter with a terrifying obstacle, offers special rewards of its own. Threatening to undermine the subject's sense of integrity and relationship to ground, the sublime gives as much if not more than it threatens to take; precisely insofar as it introduces the privative and painful, it also promises that gainful and pleasurable something that keeps the subject sharp, right on the edge of her seat. A test of endurance (for Kant, a test-drive for reason), the sublime offers the alluring thrill of surviving—living and living through—a close encounter with the abyss: the abyss of the infinite, the void, the radically other. The "as if" of the sublime—its simulation of a danger so extraordinary that it displaces the distance required for the "as if" to work—forces an encounter with a limit, most notably the limit of the subject's sense of itself and its capabilities. (Kant's discussion of the mathematically sublime pivots around the inadequacy of the imagination as ability.)[15] The sublime gives the subject a shattering experience, one that approaches and depends on an encounter with the unthinkable. Whatever it is, at its extreme, the sublime takes place by approaching the verge of madness, death, annihilation. And what to make of the appeal of such an approach amid so much madness, death, and annihilation?

War Sublime

When Kant allows for the possibility that even war might be sublime, his sketch of the conditions necessary for such an allowance relies on a given and tidy order of things. "Even war has something sublime about it if it is carried on in an orderly way and with respect for the sanctity of the citizens' rights. At the same time it makes the way of thinking of a people that carries it on in this way all the more sublime in proportion to the number of dangers in the face of which it courageously stood its ground. A prolonged peace, on the other hand, tends to make prevalent a mere[ly] commercial spirit, and along with it base selfishness, cowardice, and softness, and to debase the way of thinking of that people."[16] The masculine war sublime: power, mastery, order, the mighty yet well-ordered spectacle of a particular form of violence, that ideality of war to be "carried on in an orderly way and with respect for the sanctity of the citizens' rights." In its opposition to the anesthetizing prolonged peace and debased commercial interests of the feminine, the war sublime repeats familiar gestures of the gendered rhetoric of sovereign power. Of specific interest to me here is the very notion—and with Kant's signature as staging arena—of the aesthetics of war, of war as spectacle, of the war sublime. If Kant's portrait of the enlightening effects of war appears as a compensatory fantasy for the realities of war, all the more so today, when, as Žižek has argued, one of the residual tropes of the twentieth century, in its "passion for the real," is the incitement to violence in compensatory excess, a drive for *more* enjoyment in pleasure and pain beyond measure—more proximity, more blood, more of a rush. Such insistence on crossing a threshold takes place even within, and perhaps especially within, the hegemonic, abstracted, techno-violence legitimated in the name of war, where the distance between the covering effects of material and rhetorical prosthetics (asymmetries of materiel; the thinness of the alibi) escalates the threat of the feminine, that enervating lack in grandeur and slackening of morale that has long haunted the sublime. The related threats of anesthesia (failure to feel) and morality (the coding of that failure in ethical terms, an insinuation of guilt) create a sense of atrocity loss or sublimity in deficit. Paradoxically, the safety net required for the sublime to work (as Kant argues, there must be a certain distance from danger for the violence of the sublime to take hold, to effect the experience of pleasure and pain without a direct blow to survival) has gone too far, producing—for some—a void in the warrior's heroic rapture: avoiding the sublime experience of facing danger head on. For Žižek, the appearance of an excess of safety and distance has ripened into a pervasive insistence on crossing the line, a desire for an ever more transgressive experience of the violent encounter, for the "authentic" experience of battle, a face-to-face fight to the death.[17]

The vicissitudes of the war sublime texture a soldier's narrative from the First World War.

> I should not stress too much the horror of the war to those who actually took part in it. I know my experiences were with an exceptionally united

and successful body of men, and that to many the war was plain hell. But there was, to many of us, very much on the other side. Nor was this a joy in the actual fighting, nor a fascination with tawdry romance. There were greater things. You may say we were spiritually drugged and pathetically deluded. But never before or since have we found them. There was an exaltation, in those days of comradeship and dedication, that would have come in few other ways. And so, to those of us who had ridden with Don Quixote and Rupert Brooke on either hand, the Line is sacred ground, for there we saw the vision splendid.[18]

A "sacred ground," connected to the "exaltation" of experience (the emphasis on fellowship can also be read as a euphemistic way of pointing to a "shared" experience of death), the battlefield in this account is the singular and exceptional space of "greater things," the idealized supplement to the routine and rhetoric of life back home.

That the war introduces a limit to communicable experience, a secondary battle zone of pleasure and pain, of disavowed experience and unspeakable exceptions, is commonplace to nearly all discussions of the Great War. Benjamin, in a rhetorical question that emphasizes, ironically and as if in exasperation, that an observation so obvious should not require additional emphasis, writes, "With the [First] World War a process began to become apparent which has not halted since then. Was it not noticeable at the end of the war that men returned from the battlefield grown silent—not richer, but poorer in communicable experience?"[19]

What remains less clear, however, is the staging and scene (for and by its surviving participants, and later by historians, literary critics, and others) of the fantasy of the unspeakable, or of the notion of war as unacknowledged, suppurating wound (perhaps the wound of a no longer acceptable form of pleasure), as well as its quasi-encrypted, extant yet derailed place within language: Where, and in what form, does such experience, dispossessed of language and expelled from its recognizable forms, remain, and for whom does the "incommunicable" reveal itself as such? When Modris Eksteins, for instance, writes, "A common feeling among soldiers was that their experience at the front had created an insurmountable barrier between them and civilians. Communication with home was no longer possible. People simply could not understand what the soldiers had been through, and the soldiers themselves could not articulate their experience appropriately," the implication is split. There is a "common feeling,"[20] a truth of experience shared by the soldiers, a commonality redoubled by the impossibility of sharing their experiences with the world of noncombatants. Yet, lacking appropriate forms of expression, what becomes of such experience? In the conflict between total effacement and cathected privation, between the overwriting of repression and the return of the repetition compulsion, the experience of war becomes the site of an apocalyptic sublimity: Publicly denied but privately cherished, the "real war" returns as a no longer available form of glory, excitement, exhilaration, and loss, a secret truth (perhaps secreted away beyond recall or recognition) not only of traumatized experience, or the disavowed, unspoken experiences of shame and horror, but also of a lost sublimity, a loss of an exalted experience of a justified and heightened experience of violence, the rupture and rush of so much pleasure and pain.

That such elevated experience should take place precisely and only as lost—lost to language, to modernity, to civilized normativity—is part of the discourse of the becoming-rare of the sublime, which in any case is traditionally the scene of an already exceptional experience. In the context of the Great War, when Freud takes up the problem of the "denial of death," he argues that the war forces a turn on that negation.

> It is evident that war is bound to sweep away this conventional treatment of death. Death will no longer be denied; we are forced to believe in it. People really die; and no longer one by one, but many, often tens of thousands, in a single day. And death is no longer a chance event. To be sure, it still seems a matter of chance whether a bullet hits this man or that; but a second bullet may well hit the survivor; and the accumulation of deaths puts an end to the impression of chance. Life has, indeed, become interesting again; it has regained its full content.[21]

War is superadditive: It adds interest and restores a fullness of content. It reintroduces a "belief"—a belief in the force that binds life to death. That Freud allows for the illusion of such fullness (which Freud connects to a counterformation, the "disillusionment" of the war), suggests that the war fills a troublesome and abiding void. The missing "content," which appears here as a restored "belief"—belief in the death of the other, belief in the impossibility of escaping death through "chance"—implies that wartime from the home front provides a satisfying and needful injection. Mass death at a distance is a curative affair, an energizing intake; through magnitude of scale, the scene of war imposes just enough to present a lesson in reality ("People really die"). War, as if it were reality only in high dosage, offers a necessary and forceful sublimation—not of death but of the fear and denial of death, both of which contribute to an over- and misvaluation of life, an attachment to survival at all costs, which turns into a paralyzing neurosis. Unable to accept the necessity of death, "We dare not contemplate a great many undertakings which are dangerous but in fact indispensable, such as attempts at artificial flight, expeditions to distant countries or experiments with explosive substances. We are paralysed."[22] Masculinity's melancholia is alleviated and retrospectively defined in the apparent clarity of wartime: overattachment to life, fear of death, inability to risk life and death for the "dangerous but in fact indispensable" tasks of modern warfare. One is justified in asking whether war is produced in order to be consumed. The simplicity of the procedure, if this alone were all, would argue for the economic value of war. Freud's argument, however, is not altogether an endorsement for a symbolic expenditure of violence. The quickening effects of wartime, necessary and interest bearing as they may be, present perils of their own.

In the same essay, Freud, addressing the issue of the disillusionment wrought by the war—disillusionment as a loss of belief, falling or exposure of illusion, an injury to the ideal and image of Europe—writes of war as unprecedented threat.

> Not only is [the war] more bloody and destructive than any war of other days, because of the enormously increased perfection of weapons of attack and defence; it is at least as cruel, as embittered, as implacable as any that has preceded it. It disregards all the restrictions known as International Law, which in peace-time the states had bound themselves to observe; it ignores the prerogatives of the wounded and the medical service, the distinction between civil and military sections of the population, the claims of private property. It tramples in blind fury all that comes in its way, as though there were to be no future and no peace among men after it is over.[23]

Freud enfolds the material history of technology ("the enormously increased perfection of weapons of attack and defence") within a larger narrative in which war threatens to have become merely and entirely a force of negation and unbridled, purposeless ("blind") destruction. Structured around verbs of forceful undoing and a turning away from prior agreements and acts of synthesis (the war "*disregards* all restrictions known as International Law" and "*ignores*" the conventions, norms, and expectations established by previous wars), the passage addresses the representation of the war as unrestricted violence, positing a remainderless shattering, as if the war threatened to bring an end to all: "It tramples in blind fury on all that comes in its way, as though there were to be no future and no peace among men after it is over." Here Freud articulates a sketch of total war as a negative scenario, a catastrophic outcome that threatens to "trample" the totality of all that remains (the surviving effects of the past, history made collective in the moment of its destruction), a threat Freud reads as a negation of futurity twice over: The war acts "as though there were to be no future and no peace among men after it is over," a doubling that would cancel not only the "more" time called the future but also any meaningful differentiation between wartime and some-thing else, violence and its aftermaths. With "no peace among men," what would it mean to say that war has ended, that one could speak of a time "after it is over"? Writing in the midst of the war, Freud anticipates this impasse of ending. His provision for "ambivalence of feeling" as a possible conceptual resolution, a way of theorizing the popular discursive invest-ment in disillusionment (ambivalence, he suggests, is "a very remarkable phenomenon, and one strange to the lay public")[24] only reinscribes the difficulty: At stake is not merely the return of "interest" to life, but also, perhaps at the same time, the conflicting effects attendant upon its with-drawal or the conflict of seeing the war in an anticipatory retrospect. One might also argue that at stake is Freud's own ambivalence toward the war and Germany's place in the world of nations once it comes to an end.

Freud's rhetoric repeats, in implicit terms, the conflicting embrace of the war sublime: an elevating experience of violence, an interest bestowed by an undeniable rush and magnitude of death, particularly insofar as it presumes and keeps death at just the right distance, and, at the same time, the divided attachments at work in the idea of life "after" such an experi-ence, perhaps a growing attachment to a proximity to violence, perhaps a realization that such an attachment has long been in play. Such an attach-ment, Freud suggests, knows no end; such an attachment must come to an end. And what is the end of violence? When will the violence have come to an end? And, similarly, what of the end of the end of the denial of death? What might it mean to sustain—or not to sustain—the interest in life produced through the incursions of mass death? What do we not want from the war sublime?

The sublime has always teetered on the vanishing edge of a definition that constitutively fails to bind its object. That which might *hold up* the sublime—the grounds of its distinction and its place, the conditions that would keep such a place firmly and recognizably in place so as to allow the sublime to rise above the danger of not taking place at all—also threaten to arrest the sublime, denying it the power of movement, keeping it from the freedom to ascend, from the torsions, surges, and vibrations that make for its allure. It is well known that the sublime has always thrived on the threat of exceeding all bounds, including those that would frame its definition and location of ground. Given its historical associations with the infinite and the formless, the unimaginable and the overflowing, the terror of the inexplicable and the inexplicability of terror, it should come as no great surprise that the place of the sublime is no longer—and never has been—fully contained or successfully mastered by any one theoretical model or approach. Indeed, even while the seductive power of the sublime has so often been attributed to the characteristics of the object (Kant's objections notwithstanding) and despite a generic rhetoric that would locate sublimity in the uncontrolled might of nature or transcendent voice of god (the awesome spectacle of the natural disaster, the moralizing fantasy in which the sublime becomes, as nature's vengeance or divine justice, meaningful), the place of the sublime remains in question. The mixed responses to the proliferating images of terror today—the natural and the human disaster, the discursive danger and the ambivalent explosivity attached to certain event-names (Auschwitz, 9–11, Katrina)—only continue to work on the problem of the late sublime. The *late sublime*: the sublime of late, the sublime as it approaches and defers the cap of and end to sublimity, the sublime and the thought of the sublime (no) more.

The sublime is a discourse of verticality pitched on a void. Like the tightrope walker's dance with death, the elevation of the sublime requires a chasm, an unfathomable abyss in which to fall. The conflict of the late sublime is not between sure-footed ground and threat of engulfment, but rather between stability of ground and lack of new, ever more quickening alternatives: the framing and taming of the void, the neutralization of the disturbing threat to place and loss of ground. Yet the late sublime, to the extent that there is one, is not the end of the sublime. The late sublime is an aesthetics of sublimity at the point of exhaustion and an aesthetic experience in an age of exhaustion. What gives the notion of lateness its interest is not a return to tropes of decadence, decline, or apocalyptic endings. Rather, lateness is an effect of the very problem of ending without end—of a sense of belatedness (coming after, perhaps with a resonance of having missed out on the event) that intermixes with the suspension of totality, closure, and the reassurance of a coming or achieved rupture with the past. The late sublime emerges out of an exhaustion that is not exhaustive, an iterative lessening and draining effect, the repetition of a threat or promise to end, particularly to bring the end of all, a repetition that does not fail to fail to come to fruition. The late sublime is the inheritor of Blanchot's reading of the disappointed demand for the all-effecting turning point, the arrival of the definitive catastrophe. "The apocalypse is disappointing."[25]

The Time of Catastrophe

We insist, it seems, on living.

Virginia Woolf, *The Waves*

The historian Eric Hobsbawm has called the twentieth century the "age of catastrophe," a characterization that has become commonplace in the prolific rhetoric of global destruction (itself a compressed spatialization introduced by the first and second "world" wars) and mass death (a comparative category enabled by new media and networks of archivization, such as recorded testimony, newspaper photography, national and local museums of remembrance, and searchable databases).[26] As a generalized term, "catastrophe" broaches the collective, suggesting an epoch of inescapable violence and the violence of inescapability. At the same time, along with notions of shared inheritance, collective witnessing, and the responsibility of the survivor, the category of catastrophe introduces questions about the unspeakability, singularity, exceptionality, and incomparability of the disaster. In what language, through what demand or expectation of meaningful outcome (catastrophe is, after all, an issue of endings), is the subject of catastrophe given to speak, set to work for and against the economization of loss, death, and negativity?

Given the demand to remember past suffering, catastrophe often occasions an apotropaic logic of prevention and protection, troping futurity within the oppositional coordinates of repetition and rupture, loyalty to the past and the betrayal of departure, iterative violence and the impossibility of imagining an alternative. Catastrophe, concept-name for an age, spins the rhetoric of periodization in equivocal directions. With its connotations of explosive negativity, unredeemed violence, and unprecedented powers of destruction, catastrophe carries the burden of signifying a history that exceeds, and for that reason continues to demand, the reassuring claims of ethical closure and narrative coherence. Even as historians have sought to represent and make sense of the twentieth century's many iterations of catastrophe (indeed, already we must acknowledge the questions that persist: How many? What form of accounting and measurement would suffice?), catastrophic events (of which, not only were there many, far more than one, a multiplicity that already complicates any use of "catastrophe" as a commensurating umbrella term) accrue a differential force, threatening, one might as well say promising, to shatter the claims of reason and investment in the future. At the same time, with its intimation of sheer negativity, the blind force of catastrophe may be too much to take, and perhaps too much to hope for. "We feel that there cannot be any experience of the disaster, even if we were to understand disaster to be the ultimate experience."[27]

And yet—Blanchot's nuanced writing of the "writing of the disaster" notwithstanding—variations on and substitutes for an "experience of the disaster" are on offer all around us. Perhaps it is precisely because the disaster, as Blanchot presents it, recedes and skirts, looming at the horizon of experience and understanding, suggesting itself only in the disaster of the work, the disintegrations and openings of the space of writing; perhaps it is because the disaster splinters reason and mocks mastery ("The disaster alone holds mastery at a distance"),[28] as an intimation of the "ultimate experience," the disaster insists on being comforted, or on the idea that the spectacle of disaster should somehow comfort us.

What we want from the catastrophe is always a mixed affair: We want more and no more catastrophe. Perhaps we want for the catastrophe, insofar as it wreaks havoc with the norm, to have changed everything, a messianic turn. Perhaps we want from the catastrophe, insofar it wreaks havoc with the norm, to deliver only more of the same, not to have changed anything at all. Catastrophe, then, the anticipated but unknown end, the end of catastrophe, catastrophe as its aftermaths. And what, then, of catastrophe as the future of catastrophe? Is there a future after catastrophe? "A subject always declares meaning in the future anterior," Alain Badiou writes.[29] In putting forward his "metaphysics of catastrophe," or a metaphysics "adapted to the age of catastrophe," Jean-Pierre Dupuy has argued that we must insist on a thinking of the catastrophic event, or a making of its eventuality thinkable, such that the catastrophe is situated in the paradox of the future anterior: The catastrophe must be thought of as both inevitable and avoidable.[30] Catastrophe is the inevitable destructive event, the destiny that must be taken seriously because it is coming, because, from the perspective of the future, it is what will have taken place; catastrophe is the chance that the catastrophe might (not) have been the inevitable destructive event. "The catastrophic event is written in the future as if it were destiny, certain and with certainty, but also as a contingent accident; it might not occur, even if, in the future anterior, it appears as if it were necessary."[31] Is this not a way of imagining the worst, and of doing so in order to frighten enough, so as to induce the urgency and desire for altering destiny? Thus, for Dupuy, the future anterior is the grammar adequate to the rigors and stakes of an "ethical aporia."[32]

The future anterior has, then, ethical and aesthetic weight. For Lyotard, the future anterior is the grammar of the correct "understanding" of the sublime, that understanding he calls the postmodern. "The postmodern would be that which in the modern invokes the unpresentable in presentation itself, that which refuses the consolation of correct forms, refuses the consensus of taste permitting a common experience of nostalgia for the impossible, and inquires into new presentations—not to take pleasure in them, but to better produce the feeling that there is something unpresentable. . . . *Post-modern* would be understanding according to the paradox of the future (*post*) anterior (*modo*)."[33] Associated with a breaching of aesthetic horizons, including those of taste, legitimacy, and the limits of form, the postmodern, like the modern, which it does not simply surpass, insists on and calls attention to the contingency, fungibility, and incoherence of any "rules" that could be said to govern the work of art. Like the modern, which has long been characterized by a quest for the new, the postmodern is critical of any and all agreed-upon notions of the aesthetically significant, acceptable, and possible. For Lyotard, the postmodern names a condition, perhaps even an imperative, by which the work of art might become, through its own explosive rewriting of the rules, an "event": "The artist and the writer therefore work without rules and in order to establish the rules for what *will have been made*. This is why the work and the text can take on the properties of an event."[34] The future anterior, that grammatical mode that writes the future as past, is, Lyotard emphasizes, most interestingly understood as paradox. The structure of the "will have been" suggests a state of already-ness, a temporality of completion and decidability through which the incompletion and undecidability of the future (assuming the future to remain, in the future, other to whatever it is we can know and say about it in the present; in other words, assuming the future to remain a site of alterity) are vanquished and put to rest. And yet it is precisely such a stasis of completion and predictability of achievement—the "new," changed rules sketched out in advance and played out already—that Lyotard wants the postmodern to suspend, defer, and critique: the postmodern, a catastrophe in the making.

The paradox of the future anterior (the temporization into a projected future of some "x" that, as looked back upon from a subsequent or another future, "will have been") emerges not so much in comparison with the future present (a projection without retrospect, some "x" that "will be"), but from the future anterior and its relationship to the time of completion. The writing futurity in the mode of the future anterior anticipates the future as completed interval, the future rendered finite because seen as over, located in a past. Framed and recollected from the position of an afterwards, the future becomes future-as-past. At the same time, such differing and dividing of the future implies that the future is not at an end; the future anterior requires precisely that the future will not have been completed. By projecting (at least) "two" futures—the future-as-past and the future(s) from which that future is seen as past—the future anterior closes off and opens the future.

Whereas for Lyotard the future anterior presents the paradox of the postmodern in its anticipatory breaking (out) of form, for Derrida at stake in the future anterior is the rhetoric and temporality of an anticipatory anxiety related to the uncertainty of death's time of arrival, the impossibility of putting death behind us. Also at stake is the neutralization of the future. Derrida links this paradox to the founding structure of archivization, or the archive as it *anticipates* the future.

> Anticipation opens to the future, but at the same time, it neutralizes it. It reduces, presentifies, transforms into memory [*en mémoire*], into the future anterior and, therefore, into a memory [*en souvenir*], that which announces tomorrow as still to come. A single movement extends the opening of the future and by the same token, by way of what I would call a *horizon effect*, it closes the future off, giving us the impression that "this has already happened." I am so ready to welcome the new, which I know I'm going to be able to keep, capture, archive, that it's as if it had already happened and as if nothing will ever happen again. And so the impression of "No future" is paradoxically linked to a greater opening, to an indetermination, to a wide-openness, even to a chaos, a chasm: anything at all can happen, but it has happened already.[35]

And such a paradoxical link between projecting, claiming, grasping in advance the end of the future and some other future, some remainder, a future besides, a future that hangs in suspension of the dialectic's appropriative movement yet is also its requirement—such a paradox within the advance work of thinking, anticipating, making claims on the future is, of course, linked, one might say as its allegorical exemplum, to the anticipation of death.

> It has already happened; death has already happened. This is the experience of death. And yet, like death the event, the other, is also what we don't see

coming, what we await without expecting and without horizon of expectation. To be able to anticipate is to be able to see death coming, but to see death coming is already to be in mourning for it, already to amortize, to be able to start deadening death [*à amortir la mort*] to the point where it can't even happen anymore. It can't even happen anymore and everything has happened already. This double experience, which belongs to the structure of anticipation, to the structure of the horizon, to the structure of mourning, too, is not new, of course.[36]

Collating around the "double experience" of anticipation and its claims to the future, more than one word gathers in the attempt to think, and for Derrida to affirm, the possibility of the more than already negated "negative," a horizon of anticipation beyond or other to the work of amortization: the event, the other, the new. As for death, it can only ever be anticipated; there is no getting around it.

The "Unprecedented"

Foremost in our minds at this moment is of course the enormously increased human power of destruction, that we are able to destroy all organic life on earth and shall probably be able one day to destroy even the earth itself.

Hannah Arendt, *The Human Condition*

It has become commonplace to acknowledge that at some point during the last century the speed and scale of human history not only changed, but changed in unprecedented ways. Along with the rhetoric of the first, the new, and the never-before, the unprecedented emerges with increased, and perhaps unprecedented, range and frequency as the twentieth century negotiated an onslaught of threshold formations and an uncertain increase in drift. Registering the irreversible effects of techno-science and the delocalized futures of capitalist modernity, the unprecedented strides a tension between the unpredictable and the inevitable, writing the event as unforeseeable irruption or, alternatively, as logically necessary outcome.[37] We are often reminded of the issue of speed, of an acceleration of the rate and experience of change, a kind of velocity effect that precipitates a hastening toward inevitable yet unknown ends. The century that launches the discourse of futurology (a genre that now includes various institutionally legitimized subspecies, such as the growing discourse of risk management, as well as the financial market's trade in futures) strives to make a science of prediction, taking into account the catastrophes of the accident and the surprise. Computer-driven calculations and programs of modeling instrumentalize the desire to control the future and, in so doing, to cancel out the abeyance it holds in delay. In the drive toward the instantaneous and simultaneous, incommensurability takes shelter in monuments to eternity as the sacred becomes kitsch: The mausoleum gives over to the museum; the museum to the hotel lobby. With and against such de-sacralizations of death and distance, the century proliferates a culture of the late or vanishing sublime: Whereas Kant's sublime sacrifices the imagination to reason, the late sublime expends itself in the thrill of watching the end of the world on screen. Thus the century lays claim to a singularly unprecedented achievement: If, as is often claimed, humanity has invented, for the first time in history, the means to annihilate itself, destroy the earth, and bring an end to history, the fantasy of surviving such total destruction goes hand in hand with the logic that produces the possibility of such a "last" event. The signature mark of the twentieth-century apocalypse—the end of uncertainty, the end of pain, the end without remainder.

Yet the taming of the remainder—assimilating the rest and the future of all once and for all—is not achieved without cost. The unprecedented, and along with it the power of the new and the hope for more (more life, more energy, more time), carries the promise of surplus, extension, and profit only to the extent that it introduces the violence of rupture, destruction, and loss. "No ideology which aims at the explanation of all historical events of the past and at mapping out the course of all events of the future can bear the unpredictability which springs from the fact that men are creative, that they can bring forward something so new that nobody ever foresaw it."[38] The unbearability of the unpredictable is the threat and hope of the future, of a different future, a future all the same.

The unpredictability held by the future functions, for Arendt, as a space from which to undermine the strangling logic of totalitarian rule. Yet if the "unpredictability which springs from the fact that men are creative, that they can bring forward something so new that nobody ever foresaw it" lodges a wrench in the paranoid certainties that structure totalitarian power, it does not guarantee that there will be, always and for the rest of time, more futurity to count on. With the twentieth century's introduction of more and more powerful means of destruction, the unprecedented escalates and comes to include, in the rhetoric of futures unprecedented and the "unthinkable" nuclear event, the possibility of "no (more) future." The threat of such an unsurvivable end—the end of the future, the end of history, the end of man-as-species—takes place only as fantasy (which does not mean that it cannot happen); were such a totality of destruction to have occurred, there would be none left, no remaining language or life to speak of it, mourn it, memorialize it as event. Indeed, the negative fantasy, or unthinkable scenario, that would, for the first and last time, bring a susbsequentless end to humanity is perhaps more desirable and easier to tolerate than a scenario in which the apocalyptic event, however much of an absolute rupture with all that came before, would leave a trail of after-maths: victims, suffering remains. Moreover, as Blanchot has argued, the notion of the "end of history" is problematic in its fantasmatic and rhetor-ical investment in a fiction of totality—totality created only through and at the moment of a last and total negation.

> "The end of history." We should listen carefully to what this limit-concept allows to be said: a critical operation, the decision to put totality itself out of play, not by denouncing it but by affirming it, and by considering it as accomplished. The end of history: the total affirmation that cannot be ne-gated since negation is already included in it (just as, on the basis of the discourse that contains its own silence, no silence of this discourse can be attested to, hoped for, or dreaded).[39]

For Blanchot, the rhetorical and libidinal investment at work in the "end of history," and with it the idealization of future-no-more, is problematic because it conjures totality only at the expense of any remaining possibility for critically rethinking the problem of totality. The threat and claim of the "end of history" short-circuits a serious problem, displacing it through an end run that leaves no way out, no more room to move.

In a different register, Kant raises the question not of killing off history altogether but of unjustly hampering its "progress." When, in "What Is Enlightenment?" Kant addresses the obligation of the present precisely not to negatively limit, or unjustly constrain, the future, it is clear that he assumes *there will be* a future. For Kant, the unit-character of the future is articulated in terms of successive "generations."

> One age cannot bind itself, and thus conspire, to place a succeeding one in a condition whereby it would be impossible for the later age to expand its knowledge (particularly where it is so very important), to rid itself of errors, and generally to increase its enlightenment. That would be a crime against human nature, whose essential destiny lies precisely in such progress; sub-sequent generations are thus completely justified in dismissing such agree-ments as unauthorized and criminal.[40]

From the last part of the passage, it is clear that Kant's object is not a scenario in which the one generation threatens to destroy itself and, in so doing, to negate human life altogether. Still, Kant's argument prepares the way for the argument made two centuries later by the philosopher Hans Jonas, who, in calling for a new "ethics of the future" in the face of unprecedented threats to the present and future existence of the human as species, asserts the *"unconditional duty* for mankind to exist. . . . It is this ontological imperative, emanating from the idea of Man, that stands behind the prohibition of a *va-banque* gamble with mankind." Jonas calls for a new form of ethics, a "new ethics of responsibility for and to a distant future."[41]

Implied in Jonas's critique of the risk of the all—the gamble of *"va-banque,"* the gaming on a future that is not "ours" to risk—is the notion that we (whoever "we" are—and again, as Jonas recognizes and as Blanchot has argued, it is one of the special effects of catastrophe discourse to invoke and assume a collective precisely, and indeed only, through the threat of its destruction) owe a debt to the future, a responsibility derived from an "ontological imperative" that makes us responsible not only to our neighbors, the figures of an obligation in proximity and to community and others in the present, but also to and for an infinite and infinitely abstracted future—a "distant future." A future beyond our lives, a future after our deaths. If questioning the assumption that there should and must *be* a (human) future raises the charges of decadence and cynicism, we can at least question the genealogy of the mandate and the increased sense of urgency that surrounds the demand to protect it. How did we come to inherit so many apotropaisms of futurity, warnings and spin-offs dedicated to warding off the end of the future?

The Unprecedented, the Modern

Isn't history ultimately the result of our fear of boredom, of that fear which will always make us cherish the novelty and the spice of disaster, and prefer any misfortune to stagnation? An obsession with the unheard-of is the destructive principle of our salvation.

E. M. Cioran, *History and Utopia*

She thought that she would miss the queer, absurd show, which would go on with its antics without her, down who knew what aeons. Perhaps not very many after all; perhaps all life was before long dustily to subside, leaving the ball, like a great revolving tomb, to spin its way through space. Or perhaps the ball itself would dash suddenly from its routine spinning, would fly, would rush like a moth for a lamp, to some great, bright sun and there burst into flame, till its last drift of ashes should be consumed and no more seen.

Rose Macaulay, *Told by an Idiot*

It is a truism of the twentieth century that history had come to be driven by forces that exceed human understanding and control. Whether framed in terms of the psychological, economic, technological, or biological, or these categories together along with others, the limitations of knowledge are understood (if we can suspend the meaning of the word) to structure our relationships to the world, exerting at least as much, if not more, pressure on us as do those bits of understanding we think of as reliably our own. The recent saeculum, age of unprecedented destruction and thwarted idealization of progress, reasserts and escalates what Reinhart Koselleck has called the "aporia of progress," or the iterative fault line of modernity as it spins the future ideal according to a logic of "perfectibility." "Precisely because and so long as progress is unfinished, the chances of decay increase—admittedly, no longer read in natural metaphorics but rather in the sense of catastrophes that human beings have become capable of bringing about for themselves with the technological powers at their disposal."[42]

Catastrophe: The problem of the floating negative and the failure to determine its future, to set a fixed orbit on the future of the human and its powers of destruction, is posited both as lack and excess: lack of governing agent or sovereign structure to conquer (setting to work for profit, or, if more profitable, dissolving altogether) the foreign, the demotic, the barbaric within and without; lack of a coherent encoding and the setting to work of lack itself; similarly, for excess, that which remains unknown, outside of reason's encompassing range; forces beyond control; the proliferating buildup beyond measure or mastery of more and more data, processed only by increasingly specialized fields. The breakdown of any integral frame leaves more and more remaindered forms to spill out, threatening to return as contaminants. Catastrophic ambivalence: (no) more catastrophe.

We may generally have a sense of catastrophe as something of a turn for the worse. Catastrophe carries a negative bearing, connotations of bad events, unwanted or unfortunate outcomes. As for the idea of "outcome," although it might suggest a path of predictable causality, it also allows for the input of chance. Catastrophe, then, is not one thing or the other: success against failure, good or bad, standard or deviation. The destructive routes of catastrophe are many, given to changes of fortune and form. Catastrophe need not be biblical or effected by the caprice of the gods. Catastrophe should not be understood mechanically; it is part of catastrophe's disturbance to come without warning, scrambling reference to known coordinates. Although there may be types of catastrophe, we are not concerned with refining a genre or locking down its law. Perhaps most of all, catastrophe is whatever is the worst, the most difficult to bear. Catastrophe wrecks expectations (even for catastrophists). Catastrophe need not destroy the whole world, and indeed some catastrophes are the worst because they fail to let us leave the world behind. "'Worst' can serve as a rhetorical qualification of 'moment,' which may not be restricted or an indication of closure."[43]

If we turn to the past, catastrophe recalls a dramatic vocabulary. Etymologies, even if we have learned to be suspicious of their limits, can still be useful for a start. "Catastrophe": "Gr. overturning, sudden turn, conclusion," from "down + to turn." As for the definitions, the *Oxford English Dictionary* offers as its first two entries, "1. The change or revolution which produces the conclusion or final event of a dramatic piece," and "2. A final event; a conclusion generally unhappy . . . a disastrous end, finish-up, conclusion, upshot; overthrow, ruin, calamitous fate."[44] The interesting note here is the alternation, perhaps a relationship, between two accents—"turning" and "ending." Another source takes us further into a narrative lexicon: "*The Catastrophe.*—The catastrophe of the drama is the closing action. . . . In it the embarrassment of the chief characters is relieved through a great deed. . . . To the more recent poets, the catastrophe is accustomed to present difficulties. This is not a good sign."[45]

"Shrinking Earth"

The threat, and this is the great confinement, is having in one's head a reduced mental picture of the Earth—an Earth that is constantly flown over, traversed and violated in its real size. That shrinking Earth is destroying me for that very reason, me, the planet-man who is no longer aware of any expanse at all.

Paul Virilio, *Politics of the Very Worst*

"With technology's having seized power—a revolution this, planned by no one, totally anonymous and irresistible—the dynamism has taken on aspects not contained in any earlier idea of it and not foreseeable by any theory, Marxist or other. It now has a direction which, instead of fulfillment, *could* lead to a universal disaster, and a tempo whose frightened exponential acceleration is apt to escape every control."[46] The rhetoric of an unprecedented age: an epoch that defines itself with reference to the problem of envisioning, coding, controlling the unprecedented; that writes itself through some acknowledgment (it will have to be limited) of the problems presented by an unprecedented accrual of power-knowledge, inventions, and discoveries that, precisely in their "offer" of unprecedented power and possibilities, open onto futures unknown. The unprecedented—is it not always a question of the future? Indeed of the end of the future?

We are often reminded that the twentieth century, with its widespread proliferation of new and overlapping means of connectivity and reterritorialization (distance-spanning technologies ranging from the telephone to the high-speed train to the long-range missile to the military communications satellite, to name a few), launches an epoch of ever-increasing—and unprecedented—historical and experiential acceleration. Such a speeding up of the rate and experience of change represents, from Marx onward, a consistent paradox of capitalist modernity: The erosion of all grounds, of the material bases that would resist the hastening advancement of "everlasting uncertainty and agitation,"[47] becomes a new form of rule. Thus the tyranny of capital in its unbridled expansion generates a form of structural inevitability: Capitalism works according to a programmatic ungrounding, or the constant displacement of any priorities and logic other than its own. In a poetics I call "modernist" for its related emphases on the destructive sublimation of tradition, the undoing of all fixed forms, a ferocious, fundamentally substanceless drive toward the ever new, and, alongside such an accent on the empty force of the negative, a simultaneous affirmation of a counterforce in the critical project, one that promises a different narrative of progress, that gestures toward a new grounds for truth (for Marx, an eventual turning to "face" the truth of a new reality), Marx famously states:

> All fixed, fast-frozen relations, with their train of ancient and venerable
> prejudices and opinions, are swept away, all new-formed ones become anti-
> quated before they can ossify. All that is solid melts into air, all that is holy
> is profaned, and man is at last compelled to face with sober senses his real
> conditions of life and his relations with his kind.[48]

Splicing the intervals between input and outcome, departure and arrival, action and effect, the drive and desire for velocity ultimately hasten toward a telos of the instantaneous, zeroing out the incommensurables lodged by discontinuity, unpredictability, and the drag of delay. At the same time, emergent within the spread of industrial capitalism and the expansions of empire, the rhetoric of the unprecedented recodes the measure and meaning of distance, incrementally pushing toward a virtual negation of the very possibility of the inaccessible, or space out of reach. No (more) empty space, the end of the conquest of nature's surplus, the end of the difference of distance.

It is hardly surprising that the threat of the end of nature, one of capitalist modernity's running refrains, continues to draw energy from the shifting rhetoric of the limit. By the beginning of the twentieth century, the imminence of the end takes hold in the form of a lament over the end of an era, the near-end of capital's golden epoch of limitless expansion. The positing of such an imposing horizon of finitude often pivots on the becoming-scarce of the infinitely productive resource of the primitive: the space of the uncoded, the zone without history, the earth without writing. A limit established at the moment of its crossing, the fantasy of having saturated the globe, and thus of having newly reached the "ends of the earth," appears in various discursive forms, notably the image of cartographic saturation, the finished or filled up map of the earth.[49] At the same time, the threat of nature "no more"—no more empty space to discover, no more room to expand, no more so-called primitive accumulation— finds itself displaced only to reappear in other forms. The exhaustion of one figure of the more-than-finite, of the infinitely giving resource (nature, abundance of earth), is both acknowledged and deferred. By the end of the century, the location, name, and nature of the gift of nature has shifted: The primitive becomes the indigenous; colonialism's territorialization of the reserve is transvalued into a concern over the preservation of common inheritance; the investment in mapping the horizontal plane of the earth's surface is redirected to the verticality of heights and depths. In the context of such shifts, the threat of the end of nature returns in catastrophic scenarios of the unprecedented, unsurvivable catastrophe.

The category of the unprecedented often occurs as a kind of precritical catchword for the promises and dangers of the more ideologically laden, contentious category of the modern, with which it shares the implied connotation not only of the new, but of the "new new," a doubling of the new between the now and the not-yet. For the modern, this doubling implies a tension between the modern as a grammatical shifter that calls into being the cutting edge of a contemporary present (the empty moment of the now, always available for reuse) and the modern as evaluative, a historical and critical category that designates a notion of periodicity (the modern as not only coeval with the rise of capitalism in the West but the very discourse in which it becomes possible to speak of making a cut into history, to start anew starting now, the rhetoric of an epoch that would refashion itself in terms of its very own). This tension between the modern as a performative that projects a retrospection in the mode of the future perfect (if the modern privileges the irruptive actuality and creative originality of the present as it inaugurates a new future, the effects of that founding intervention will depend on—will have to have come from—a subsequent future) and as a constative that would refer to a preexisting, recognizable, and accomplished period, event, or ideology (modernity in the West; modern literature; modernism as distinct from and even defined by postmodernism) demonstrates the difficulty, interest, and effect of the modern. Even as it is invoked to name the presence of an achieved ethos or aesthetic ("modernism") or historical-political era and established set of values ("modernity"), the modern—caught in the aporia between a singular and repeatable now, as well as in the double bind wherein the affirmation of the present's transformative power risks reducing the future to more of the same—calls into question the ontological priority and stability of the modern as such.

Like that of the modern, the category of the unprecedented vacillates between an absolute yet empty present (the unprecedented as the singularity and chronological privilege of any given moment as it somehow exceeds and differs from all those that came before it) and the uncertain significance of an event so previously unthinkable (a condition of relative privation and negativity that can be established only later, after the fact) that its taking place emerges as other to and without place within the totality of any prior symbolic system or epistemic horizon. Indeed, it is with the very calculation and thought of totality that the unprecedented takes issue, calling into question the possibility of rendering history and meaning—past, present, and future—on the model of a completed whole.

Emerging as a step beyond all prior horizons of expectation, the unprecedented introduces, and possibly more than once, a schizoid, counter-dialectical logic of the event. As that which lacks comparability—and perhaps even introduces an essential in-comparability—in relation to any and all prior history (for example, to the extent that it can be presented as an example, the event of the Holocaust), the unprecedented appears to destabilize teleologies of progressive development, including those dialectical models for which the moment of exception, as the negative on the way to an inevitable sublation, would not so much subtract from as it would augment and extend the certitudes of reason and the will to knowledge.

Exceeding the limits of the past in its self-certainties and claims to absolute knowledge, the event without precedent might, if taken seriously, disrupt the very idea of totality, lodging itself, perhaps like a bone in the throat of any past or future digestive system, at the lethal limit of what the system can handle—what it can grasp or hold onto without ceasing to function. Rising up from the nonplace of an unanticipated alterity that refuses seemly recognition and scrambles the proprieties of form, the unprecedented takes place only and precisely to the extent that it threatens not to—that its destabilizing, irruptive appearance remains "stuck," inscribed but not processed, a borderline case of the lived-impossible.

Just as the modern asserts the cutting edge of the "contemporary," the unprecedented is perched uncomfortably on an epistemo-temporal shoal, teetering between a past in which it has no place and a future in which this peculiar distinction—of being entirely out of place, of taking place by lacking place-as-precedent—will have become obsolete. As we have learned from the story of the twentieth-century avant-garde, the lifetime of radical edge-formations—the singularities of the illegible and the new, the ground-breaking and even earth-shattering situations which, as Lyotard would have it of the postmodern (and for him, truly and properly Kantian) sublime, art broaches "the unpresentable in presentation itself"—the power of such disruptive forces, in their seductive allure and hint of gainful dispossession, is in no way immune to the dominant drive-structure of capital. The outer limit is never so far from the center that its "surplus" appeal cannot be brought home, domesticated as fetish, hung up, and made to signify. However exotic or repulsive, the illegible takes shape within frame, the "outsider" remains well within range; the unprecedented is brought to account.[50]

The rhetoric of the unprecedented asserts at least two organizing preoccupations. The first emphasizes unprecedented systematization and totality, or the becoming homogenous of a world increasingly experienced, represented, and calculated *as one*. According to this line of argument, which drifts ever closer to the threat and promise of finitude (its figure is that of the "shrinking earth"), under the increasing dominance of industrial capitalism and the expansions of empire, technologies of spatial and graphic communication (for physical transport, the train, automobile, airplane; for language and images, the telegraph, telephone, radio, and eventually other tele-technologies such as the television, the computer, and the internet) rewrite the measurement and effects of geographic distance, bringing the far near (though, as Heidegger argues, not necessarily bringing us any nearer to the concept nearness).[51] Technologies of distance-spanning, accompanied by an unprecedented shift in the speed of connection, or the amount of time required for transmission, serve, as Marx argues, the interests of capital. As it drives toward unlimited expansion, capital presupposes and creates the terms of the world-as-one. "The tendency to create the world market is directly given in the concept of capital itself. Every limit appears as a barrier to be overcome." Capital, as it spins out its lines of credit and abstractions of value, writes the "annihilation of space by time."[52]

The shift toward faster, speedier mechanisms for the transport of people, goods, and signs produces qualitative change as well, or change in the conceptualization and the occurrence of change itself. Everything can hinge on an instant. Thus, for example, Virginia Woolf's famous statement "that on or about December, 1910, human character changed"—which, for all its arbitrariness, finds it necessary to go so far as to speak of the "all" of "human" as such—a totality as encompassing and qualitatively textured as one can imagine.[53] Whatever "human character" might mean, it would be difficult to conceive of a quantitative calculation of its difference from one moment to the next. It is precisely through this kind of resistance to any third term required for a logic of commensurability that the rhetoric of the unprecedented maintains its interest. The unprecedented, like the incommensurable, measures change and thinks difference at the limit of already existing indexes of sameness; the category that would assimilate the "unprecedented" to a prior series or comparable event, making it merely one "more" instance of the same even in its iterative difference, might, finding precedent for the unprecedented, render the unprecedented less troubling—or for that matter less promising. At the same time, it is not obvious what it would mean to insist that the unprecedented lack any chronologically prior iteration, that it be utterly resistant to any established register of the event or any accomplished index of meaning. Such an emphasis on the unprecedented as the illegible, as that which shatters the very possibility of categorization at the moment of its appearance, raises the question of stabilizing the unprecedented "itself" into a kind of uniform logic, a standard of difference and rupture, placing it within the bounds of definition on the order of a concept.

The "shrinking earth" hypothesis is a peculiar late nineteenth-century fantasy: no more remaining "free" space, no more land to "discover."

Within the narrative of increasing systematization and totality, or the be-
coming-one of the earth as "world," the borderline that would distinguish
the remaining, next, and final "last frontier," a territorial zone of the unassimilated and the worlds apart, is incrementally, and repeatedly, displaced
and enclosed. By the close of the nineteenth century, the colonial imaginary exhibits nostalgia for the age of discovery, with its fantasy of the
"rest" of the earth as surplus remainder lying in wait for conquest. The
newly actualized technologies of speed and transport, along with an ever-
increasing mediatization of actuality, combine to create an ambivalent fantasy of the world as *one*, a world in which earth, "shrinking" into an imagined unity of finite territorialization, becomes a testing ground for
thinking the measure and meaning of spatial in-completion: How many
times and in how many ways can we cross the last boundary, incorporating
and extending the final frontier, reaching and taking leave from the "ends
of the earth"? A commonplace of early twentieth-century colonial geogra-
phy, the fiction of an earth "filled up" on the map, registers the structure
of the cartographer's desire, the desire (not) to have completed the map.
"Of late it has become a commonplace to speak of geographical exploration as nearly over. . . . [T]here is scarcely a region left for the pegging
out of a claim of ownership." At stake for this British geographer in 1904
is the negotiation for power over the political remainder.[54]

"There was a time when we had a planet but not a world. There were
several worlds. One was on the Mediterranean. A second was in India.
Columbus found a third. There were still others. Now there is but one—
mechanically. And it is becoming more contracted every day."[55] In imagining a world system, this author, writing in 1927, links the image of an
achieved, integrated totality to an ambivalent fantasy of control through
mapping and visualization, positing "an unconscious and inevitable effort
toward world crystallization . . . an unconscious groping toward a controlled integration of world industry. Whether this will kill or make us
depends apparently on whether or not we can control it. To control a thing
we first must see it. It must be visualized."[56] Such macrological accounts
emphasize the epistemic, spatial saturation of the globe by a dominant,
systematic ("mechanical") movement toward capitalist hegemony, a totality for which there remain no "others"—no other worlds to conquer, no
other legitimate or viable systems (notably, communism). At the same
time, the problem of mapping and control sounds a note of anxiety, a
negative fantasy of the future not as achieved or static accomplishment,
but rather as imperiled, hazardous unknown. The threat of an uncontrolled and possibly uncontrollable "mechanism" reiterates an older the-
matic in which capitalism's promise of ineluctable, imperial dominance

threatens to turn back upon its beneficiaries in the form of headless, inhuman technicity, a late form of the promethean double bind.

The trope of the "shrinking earth," like the refrain of speed, spins on
many axes and in more than one direction. For Rudyard Kipling, poet of
empire, the enclosure of the distant was both wondrous and a matter of
course. In "Some Aspects of Travel," a speech he presented to the Royal
Geographical Society in 1914, Kipling addresses contemporary changes in
the material conditions of travel (the steamship, the motorcar, the airplane), but his primary interest is in what one might call the psychological
space and language of travel, or the way the traveler imagines and represents the experience of travel as if to himself, or travel as "visualized" in
the "mental sign-talk."[57] Kipling's interest is in mapping changes in sensory cartographics, of tracking the shifting normative forms of the traveler's "impressions," or the immediate and yet, more and more as time goes
on, already mapped, one might say pre-prepared, experience of the spatially new. Indeed, the (by now common) tension in which travel strides
the possibility and impossibility of the unplanned encounter, of the encounter as and with the unknown, appears in Kipling's language as he
considers the coming disappearance of any and all unmapped space, or any
space that would remain, in any meaningful sense, somehow off limits,
beyond the fully cleared path of achieved access, the marked path of the
already mastered. Thus he states,

> One must remember that, in a few years, most of our existing methods of
> transport, together with the physical and mental emotions that accompany
> them, will be profoundly changed. The time is near when men will receive
> their normal impressions of a new country suddenly and in plan, not slowly
> and in perspective; when the most extreme distances will be brought within
> the compass of one week's—one hundred and sixty-eight hours'—travel;
> *when the word "inaccessible" as applied to any given spot on the surface of the*
> *globe will cease to have any meaning.* I present myself to-night, then, as in
> some sort a recorder of experiences which are on the eve of being
> superseded.[58]

On the threshold of "being superseded": Kipling presents himself as a
witness to a vanishing present, to changes in the experience of "experiences." What is particularly interesting here is the shifting presentation
and meaning (or lack of meaning) of the "inaccessible"—in other words
of a notion of the limit, of a sense of a geo-psycho-cartographic remainder,
of a space that would remain "off limits," beyond bounds, unavailable for
interiorization. Such a space, signified by the "word 'inaccessible' as ap-
plied to any given spot on the surface of the globe," initially posits the

availability (soon to be no more) of the uncharted geo-surface: the ground that awaits inscription. The "surface of the globe"—where is the surface and what borderline defines it? Kipling presents the "surface" as a one-dimensional plane ("any given spot") whose finitude—the exhaustion and becoming meaningless of the word "inaccessible"—has been firmly established. As fully explored and framed totality, it represents the achievements of empire and its accumulated cartographic knowledge.[59] At the same time, it represents the greatest instability, the nearness of every risk and threat unknown. "Month by month the Earth Shrinks actually, and, what is more important, in imagination. We know it by the slide and crash of unstable material all around us. For the moment, but only for the moment, the new machines are outstripping mankind."[60]

In our own time, the tension between a discourse of the world as system, as governed (even and especially in the breach) by a political-economic macrologic that could contain and account for "all" of the whole world, of history as a whole, and a discourse in which the world appears neither as one nor as the multiple of a fractured totality but rather through the work of supplementarity as always something else, something like the form of that which remains as yet without form—this tension reappears in the thinking of the event of total destruction, the event that would bring an end to all. According to the insatiable logic of inclusion and the writing of all-ness as totality, such an event is thinkable and predictable, and perhaps even desirable, in the form of finality and all-out finitude: projections of species-cide, the total destruction of the human species whether through accident or intention, whether through human or inhuman means. Such total destruction can be thought of as the emptying out of apocalypse, or apocalypse without reserve or remainder, the end of the world without the redemptive gains of divine judgment and heavenly reward. The paradoxical all-ness of such scenarios emerges in the projected retrospection of a remainderless world, a singular event of the end of the world.[61]

In the face of the end of difference—one thinks of Victor Segalen's rhetoric of the end of diversity and the decline of the exotic—modernism carries the peculiar charge of being linked with the "shrinking earth" and its "leveling effects."[62] Thus Erich Auerbach, in his famous essay on modernism, "The Brown Stocking," reads Virginia Woolf's *To the Lighthouse* as a new form of freedom and realism of psychological truth (the form of "multipersonal representation of consciousness," he argues, evinces "consciousness in its natural and purposeless freedom," a transcendental-naturalism for which "exterior events have actually lost their hegemony").[63]

Yet by the end of his essay he has returned to history's strictures, asserting a narrative of literary-historical development in which the novel, unlike its characters, answers to "exterior events."

> It is easy to understand that such a technique [the "reflection of multiple consciousnesses"] had to develop gradually and that it did so precisely during the decades of the first World War period and after. The widening of man's horizon, and the increase of his experiences, knowledge, ideas, and possible forms of existence, which began in the sixteenth century, continued through the nineteenth at an ever-faster tempo—with such a tremendous acceleration since the beginning of the twentieth that synthetic and objective attempts at interpretation are produced and demolished every instant. The tremendous tempo of the changes proved the more confusing because they could not be surveyed as a whole.[64]

Auerbach hits several significant notes in this passage: increased acceleration (given added emphasis by his own speeding up and contraction of the intervals of time), accumulated routes of access to more and different experiences, and, rather than an end of difference, a sense of increased complexity such that the synthetic no longer seems to hold. (The last note will return in Edward Said's definition of modernism, as I demonstrate in the pages to follow.) As Auerbach's argument goes on, however, the tension between expansion and contraction, incommensurability and homogenization grows more marked.

> The spread of publicity and the crowding of mankind on a shrinking globe sharpened awareness of the differences in ways of life and attitudes, and mobilized the interests and forms of existence which the new changes either furthered or threatened. In all parts of the world cries of adjustment arose; they increased in number and coalesced.

As Auerbach goes on to associate these tensions with the First World War and its aftermath, including the rise of fascism in Europe, he returns to the subject of literature, redrawing the link between fragmentations of form ("ruthlessly subjectivistic perspectives") and historical uncertainty ("a Europe unsure of itself, overflowing with unsettled ideologies and ways of life, and pregnant with disaster"). And then again, as if in imitation of the tensions he describes, he insists that the literary not be reduced to a symptom of the times. Rather, the new element of modern literary works, as represented by Woolf's novel, is "to put the emphasis on the random occurrence, to exploit it not in the service of a planned continuity of action but in itself." And, again in reversal, the random is itself representative, a way of writing that gives voice to "the elementary things which men in general have in common. It is precisely the random moment which is comparatively independent of the controversial and unstable orders over which men fight and despair. . . . The more it is exploited, the more the elementary things which our lives have in common come to light."[65] In this dialectical movement toward the new, where the new becomes representative of something already present yet only now finding its articulation, Auerbach concludes, "There are no longer even exotic peoples," thus returning us to the discourse of "leveling" ("an economic and cultural leveling process is taking place"). From the shattering of synthesis to the leveling of difference, Auerbach shuttles between the catastrophe of fragmentation to the catastrophe of fascism. Between them is the uncertain future of politics, the future of the very possibility of uncertainty.

Auerbach's ambivalent ending sets the tone for the chapters that follow, in which I continue to read the writing of catastrophe and the challenges it poses for the competing imperatives of synthesis and resistance to form.

CHAPTER 2

Virginia Woolf: Reading Remains

When, for the first time in the history of the world, one has at hand
the material power to put an end to this history and this world, one
has already departed historical space. The change of epoch has
occurred. This can be simply expressed: henceforth the world is a
barracks that can burn.

You seem to rejoice in this. But are you sure it's the first time? Perhaps
you've forgotten the Bible. . . .

Then the fire came from above. Today it comes from here below.

—MAURICE BLANCHOT, "On a Change of Epoch"

One might want to forgive modernist criticism its recurring preoccupation
with war. I say this to advance my sympathies, to lend common cause with
the impossible task of historicizing a discourse that typically, if such generic description can hold, wants to reinvent itself by rejecting the unmanageable weight and unprofitable inheritance of history. There is indeed
something irritating yet inevitably seductive about the contradictions and
complexity of the modernist moment, a densely turbulent, contested periodizing category that coincides, whatever the instability of its dates, with
the proliferation of all manner of unprecedented achievements, many of
them the destructive, scandalous (though some claim predictable, even inevitable) events of an era in which the spectacle of exceptional violence and
the rhetoric of indefensible horror became a form of scoring normality.

The First World War intensified the ambivalent charge of the unprecedented. The war's headlining phrase, the "war to end all wars," articulates
the fantasy of the unprecedented as both first and last, as an event of war
so epochal that it would, unlike all past wars, become the first war in history to bring an end to the history of war. Thus the unprecedented would
belong to the past (as the "last" iteration in a history of violence, the

final war) by becoming the inaugural event in a new history, a history of everlasting peace. At the same time, such radical stasis of violence, the complete and certain containment of hostilities implied by such an end, is bound up with a less promising image of cessation. The projected ideal of the "war to end all wars" carries a threat of all-encompassing finality, a totality of violent negation that would cut the phrase short: Rather than the brightening outlook of a beginning, the start of worldwide peace, the issue of the last battle would be the annihilating end of all future ends and beginnings, the truncating cut without issue, the last negation and event without remainder, the "war to end—all."[1]

At stake in the aporia of such lastness is nothing short of everything, the totality of the world, the end of civilization, the end of futurity, the death of the human. As the idiom of the century—with its many returns of the "unthinkable" event—might remind us, the fantasy of the last event, and with it the end of all human life, language, and memory, rests on an impossible claim of the limit: The threat of the very end of futurity, the negation of survival, and the death of the last witness projects an appropriative claim of totality that would take with it not only the possibility of its own negation but also that of its affirmation, for who or what would remain to attest to such an unspeakable, unprecedented, and subsequentless event?

The aporia of lastness, of living to survive the unsurvivable event, takes a turn at the moment new forms of the technological present both superhuman and posthuman narratives of finitude and deterritorialized, disembodied being. In his lithograph of 1882, "L'oeil, comme un ballon bizarre se dirige vers l'infini [The eye, like a strange balloon, mounts toward infinity]," Odilon Redon combines technologies of flight (in the verticality of the balloon as well as through the optical drive) with a logic of inertia, senselessness, and death (Figure 1).[2] If the aerial vehicle, like the extended rays of an enormous sight machine, is a figure of "transport" into the limitless vertical universe, its orientation requires that the earth remain within the visual field. This is possible for the viewer, but only because Redon skews the horizon, placing us both on earth and above it. This is an image of the end of sight, an eyeball driven by a corpse. A playful intimation of the posthuman horizon.

Anticipations of War

With comparatively less room for play, as unprecedented event, the war to end all wars carries with it two competing apocalyptic rotations. The

Figure 1. Odilon Redon, "L'oeil, comme un ballon bizarre se dirige vers l'infini (The Eye Like a Strange Balloon Mounts Toward Infinity)." Lithograph, 1882. The Museum of Modern Art, New York. (Digital Image © The Museum of Modern Art/Licensed by SCALA / Art Resource.

notion of the coming war as the last war charges itself with a misleading *either-or*: either the end of the history of war or the end of history tout court. As in the twisted logic of the forced choice, the demand implied by the phrase, "war to end all wars," is hardly a choice at all. If the fictive collectivity called "civilization," the quasi subject that is created precisely through the threat of its demise, were to fight and win the last and therefore the greatest of wars, the issue of forgoing war in the future would remain unresolved; in the escalation from "fight now or be killed later," from a restricted to general economy of death, only the latter would, in fact, guarantee a nonrepetition of the lethal blackmail implied by the threat. (Or, as Kant writes, so long as war permits of those "dishonourable stratagems" that threaten to end in the "vast graveyard of humanity as a whole," the idea of "perpetual peace" is plausible only in the form of perpetual nothingness, or the meaningless rest of humanity's self-inflicted extinction.)[3]

As early as the St. Petersburg Declaration of 1868, technology began to assert multiple threats to humanity, not least of them the anxiety induced by the specter of the becoming-uncivilized of warfare, a fantasy of an uncivilized future that projects (and temporally displaces) the threat of a history driven not by the ideals of enlightened nations but by an uncontrolled, unlimited, irreversible takeover of a viral and inhuman technicity.[4]

"This is already the vastest war in history. It is war not of nations, but of mankind. It is a war to exorcise a world-madness and end an age."[5] The notion of such an epoch-breaking, world-remaking exorcism will seek to maintain, at all costs, the meaningfulness of the war. H. G. Wells's anticipatory writing of the Great War as a "war to exorcise a world-madness and end an age" places hope in the eventuality of outcome and ending, a definitive conclusion to an "age" defined by the escalating threats of global unreason ("world madness") and increased violence ("the vastest war in history"). The rhetoric of "exorcism" suggests that the war will, in the end, prove to have been worth it, that the end will have justified the means, an economy of errancy beyond precedent: Beyond the suspension of hostilities, the coming peace will introduce and sustain a newly concerted articulation of value, the scarcity value of futurity. A world sharing meaning in the threat of its wake, the future of the future hinges on revolution and arrest: From madness, the end of madness; in violence, the end of violence.

That the Great War did not, in fact, inaugurate any such decisive future does not obviate a consideration of its rhetorical status as unprecedented, epochalizing event. Memorialized as the first war to spread over, saturate, discursively coordinate, and threaten to destroy the world "as a whole," the Great War's dubious "greatness" represents an escalation in the scale and experience of warfare, a shift precipitated by the accumulated development of new and more powerful technologies of destruction. Although the war's escalation in the means of violence (both in terms of new forms of materiel and an increased capacity to produce, stockpile, and transport them) does not reach the explosive, apocalyptic resonances brought about with the end of the Second World War and the initiation of the nuclear age, it does escalate the stakes of an already existing anxiety over the uncertain outcome of the dialectic of technological progress. Dominating nature, homo faber creates the tools for harnessing its power, sheltering himself from exposure (to the elements, the other, the unknown), domesticating those forces, whether coded as natural or social, that threaten to interrupt or derail his plans for a planned and rationalized future. Harnessed for capital and empire, technology as standing reserve asserts unprecedented power, projected and arrested in the threat of inertial lethality. Percolating in Wells's notion of "a war to exorcise a world-madness" is the possibility of the war-as-exorcism gone awry: Rather than purging its object or containing the evil, the means of destruction, in themselves a sign and symptom of "world-madness" (is not imperialism a "world-madness," a madness for annexation and dominance over the rest of the world?), threaten to exceed all predictive power and known limits.

In its most extreme and explosive combustion, the power of technology to exceed any human future or survivable outcome, the unproductive cessation of hostilities takes the form (or, in a sense, the nonform, the total dissolution of any order of form) of total human annihilation, the end of history as species death, habitat destruction, universal extinction of life on earth. In Horkheimer and Adorno's later formulation of the limit case, "The human capacity for destruction promises to become so great that— once this species has exhausted itself—a *tabula rasa* will have been created. Either the human species will tear itself to pieces or it will take all the earth's fauna and flora down with it."[6] Demonstrating the inhuman at work within assertion of the human, Horkheimer and Adorno present species death as inevitable, the eventual outcome of capitalism's destructive dialectic. Their unsentimental, nonapologetic insistence on such an inevitability runs counter to the century's liberal-humanist response to the danger of an uncertain relationship between technology and humanity's future. In this regard, the remarks of George Bernard Shaw are exemplary. For Shaw, "The one danger before us that nothing can avert but a general raising of human character through the deliberate cultivation and endowment of democratic virtue without consideration of property and class, is the danger created by inventing weapons capable of destroying civilization faster than we produce men who can be trusted to use them wisely."[7] There is more than one "danger" here: the promethean peril as technological determinism (in the form of an inability to fully determine or control the uses of technology), a rule-by-weaponry that threatens to surpass and destroy the human altogether; the failure of democracy, a perilous possibility in which the urgency for speed toward completion of the goal ("a general raising of human character") combines with the residual strictures of hierarchy, power, and values imposed through deliberate authority ("the deliberate cultivation and endowment of democratic virtue without consideration of property and class") to suggest the uncertainty and violence lurking within the democratic cure.

Thus, well before the historical advent of the atomic bomb, the threat of its explosive power and symbolic double bind: In the name of the future of civilization, techno-science goes forward, while the idea of weapons proffered as insurance against barbarism is based on the horrifying promise that they just might destroy the world (a promise that turns tactical in the apotropaic logic of "mutually assured destruction"). Even before the start of the nuclear age, the notion that civilized warfare was becoming impossible, or that there was an expanding contradiction between the means of warfare and the purported values of a civilized world, had already begun to take off. H. G. Wells's novel *The World Set Free*, first published in 1914, writes a fictional account of atomic warfare that begins, "The history of mankind is the history of the attainment of external power," an introductory frame appropriate to the novel's didactic tale of a future destroyed by the explosive asymmetry between technological advances and the limited progress of human insight and self-control. "Certainly it seems now that nothing could have been more obvious to the people of the early twentieth century than the rapidity with which war was becoming impossible. And as certainly they did not see it. They did not see it until the atomic bombs burst in their fumbling hands."[8]

Wells's anxious plea for coming to terms with technology, or more precisely for overcoming its false allure, is articulated in the hope that collective governance will, in the negative aftermath of an initial and nearly species-annihilating failure, prove more persuasive than the destructive history of empires at war. All the same, the horrifying spectacle of the latter lends an appeal of its own, as Wells, like other early writers of what would eventually be called science fiction, sets it to work with didactic purpose. For Wells, literature was made to serve the functional demands of "scientific prophecy."[9] "Everything that has every existed or will ever exist is here—for any one who has eyes to see."[10] The language of vision Wells uses here links him to a tradition of prophecy as privileged, prior insight and suggests a model of revelation and interpretation—a future that is both already visible and waiting to be exposed, uncovered, made (more) clear. As prophecy, literature becomes the supplement to an already decided, fully knowable field of history. Yet, clearly, Wells's sense of urgency and salvational appeal carries the anxiety of a burden, assumed by one who sees what others do not, one whose vision extends all the way to the future of the end of the universe. And what Wells sees is a future of violence, warfare at the brink of species-life.

Along the figurative lines of a hostile takeover of central command by foreign agents (sometimes called the unconscious), the paralysis effect in modern warfare preys upon the nation through its operating system, threatening a sneak attack at the "heart" by way of the inorganic body, the prosthetic brain and its communicating relays. In "Aerial Machines and War," a lecture delivered at Aldershot Military Society in 1910, Lord Montagu of Beaulieu discusses the military scenario in which a continental enemy, armed with a dirigible fleet and projectile explosives, could, in addition to destroying naval stations and other military sites, make an attempt to "paralyse the heart of the nation by attacking certain nerve centres in London, the destruction of which would impede or entirely destroy the means of communication by telephone, telegraph, rail, and road."[11] Lord Montagu's lecture, delivered just before aerial warfare became a material possibility, is, in a very strict sense, a call to arms. Noting that "our government here [as opposed to the Continental powers] seems as yet to have hardly realized the importance of the question of aerial warfare," he closes his address with a prophecy of admonition, "The day is not far distant when England will have to be something besides nominal mistress of the seas."[12]

Montagu's rhetoric anticipates the future of war as an asymmetry between air power, which promises horizontal speed, vertical mobility, and concentrated means of force (at this point, the dominant term is still that of the explosive projectile rather than the bomb), and the territorial locatedness of life on the ground. Recognizing that international law has agreed "that commercial towns may not be attacked or the ordinary means of civilization of a nation destroyed by explosives dropped from above," Montagu nonetheless concludes that such laws tend to "fall to the ground, for there is no power behind them able to enforce them." This argument stands on a logic of historical continuity in which the past, or the past as it is selectively represented for the purposes of gaining the argument (and thereby provoking an intervention in the present), is taken as a reasonable model for predicting, or simply thinking, the future (if, in the past, international law has neither governed nor protected a nation's stratagems of war . . .).[13]

Montagu's lecture consistently acknowledges a gap between the governing logic of historical precedent and the future effects of new aerial technologies. The gap comes down to this: If aerial warfare is to be fundamentally different from what is already known to be possible, the difference will be annulled, negated by assimilation into a discourse governed by the limits of "civilised nations." While international law is said to be unreliable because unenforceable, Montagu extends his faith toward a different kind of resolution to the unmanageable and unforeseeable, or the eventual—and eventually intolerable—future of war: "I have no doubt that eventually the transport of troops on a large scale will be possible by means of the air. In this case, war will be made much more horrible by the constant possibility of unforeseeable attack from above, and the result may well be that the era of the fighting aeroplane by thousands might be the prelude to the end of all fighting so far as civilized nations are concerned."[14]

*　*　*

The illusion of a world so shaped that it echoes every groan, of human beings so tied together by common needs and fears that a twitch at one wrist jerks another, where however strange your experience other people have had it too, where however far you travel in your own mind someone has been there before you—is all an illusion. We do not know our own souls, let alone the souls of others.

Virginia Woolf, *On Being Ill*

We have done our best to piece out a meagre summary from the charred fragments that remain; but often it has been necessary to speculate, to surmise, and even to make use of the imagination.

Virginia Woolf, *Orlando*

The splintering topoi of modernity are well known. Tropes of fragmentation, anomie, disillusionment, and disenchantment constitute dominant notes of modernity's rhetoric of privation, an ambivalent characterization of the modern as an experience of loss: loss of totality, tradition, ground; loss of any stable or meaningful relation to location and space of dwelling, particularly to that primal, or more often "primitive," then also "mythic," ur-dwelling recalled in the breach, from the displacement of a permanent uprooting, an insistent longing for the once-but-no-longer—the loss of earth, nature, ancestral abode. Abandoned to a "universal homesickness," as Lukács has described the normative, ineluctable pathology of the modern, the experience of modernity as radical ungrounding, for all its threat of shattering negativity, nevertheless gathers itself around at least one centralizing logic, the dominant logistics of capital. When, in his famous prose image of liquid-in-dispersal, Marx figures the structural logic of capitalism as a sublimating disappearance of solidity ("All that is solid melts into air"), the loss of the solid, or the irreversible becoming-abyssal of all prior forms of continuity, foundation, and meaning, does not imply a complete meltdown of any and all bases for comprehending reality, as the marxian terminology would continue to have it, objectively. Thus Marx will insist on holding against the spreading disorder of capitalism, or capitalism in its crisis-driven entropic drive ("Melting is an entropic process *par excellence*"), the alternative promise of a coming utopian order.[15] It is in this sense, and by way of the future, that modernity will hold out the promises of progress, salvation, and the affirmative possibility of meaning more than accumulated erosion, more than the empty accounting of loss alone.

Similarly, it is not uncommon for the story of modernism to be told in terms of a dialectics of negativity and redemption, breakdown and renewal, loss and compensation. According to one version, modernism emerges from a wide experience of historical rupture, indeed from that confluence of historical forces in which the very idea of rupture becomes, paradoxically, the dominant ideological and rhetorical topos that defines, and in a sense holds together, the representation of an epoch. Age of uncertainty, upheaval, and disillusionment, the early twentieth century intensifies the dis-ordering contradictions of modernity, quickening the dual drives of capitalism, expansion and destruction. Such a logic of quickening is itself divided between an all-encompassing, assimilative system, with a related emphasis on a structural, teleological model of inevitability and development, and a less predictable score for which disruption and disintegration, irreducible to any derived concept of the negative, are neither awaiting nor resisting incorporation into a general economy. Noting this tension, we can ask how modernism registers—as response, symptom, critique—the competing turns of such quickening negativity, and what it makes of the place and possibilities for art in and against a history of rupture.

Modernism has been understood as an aesthetics of symbolic compensation and substitutive coherence, an imaginative "holding together" of meaning and mastery in the face of worldly turbulence, disintegration, and incoherence. Thus Edward Said reads modernism as both acknowledgment of and resistance to the breakdown of colonialism's synthetic imaginary, its ever-mounting failure to subordinate the rupturing effects of difference through centralizing narratives of imperial conquest. In Said's rendering, whereas (and, in a sense, precisely to the extent that) imperialism had once sought to repress the uncertain, destabilizing effects of its encounter with alterity, modernism—particularly its ironizing appropriations of tradition and its staging of an "encyclopedic" or all-encompassing horizontal aesthetics—registers the emergence of a "desperate attempt at a new inclusiveness."[16] For Said, modernism represents a version of the return of the repressed, in which what returns is the belated, symbolic recognition of the place of the other, the other in an impossible place, the disfiguring nonplace of exclusion and refusal. Said understands modernism's attempt to suspend worldly and formal hierarchies as a substitutive effort to replace the "once-possible" ideology of empire with that of aesthetic form. Modernism offers "a form that draws attention to itself as substituting art and its creations for the once-possible synthesis of the world empires."[17]

For Said, the story of modernism is that of an aesthetic solution to a wider historical crisis, the dissolution of empire. Faced with the breakup of prior narratives of coherence, modernism, Said argues, responds by holding onto, and indeed claiming all the more as its own, the possibilities of synthesis and totality. Such claims for the power and autonomy of the work of art, Said suggests, can be as critical as they are conservative; extending the sphere of art over and in the place of (now contested) political ideologies and regimes of power, the modernist work (he gives as exemplary cases the names of Woolf, Conrad, and Joyce), if it is not merely to repeat the contradictions of the past, but rather replace them (and thus, inevitably, repeat them as well), must evince a critical cunning, a measure of distance and difference. Said will call this modernism's "irony."

At stake within Said's argument is the status of modernism as response. In a very loose sense, the dialectical structure of Said's argument reads modernism as a response to a prior and historically irreversible disruption or negation (the falling apart of a centralizing force, the coming into question of the synthesizing logics of empire). And, as symptomatic response and substitutive synthesis of its own, modernism somewhere carries over the negated term, the weight of a dead past, a closed story that is not quite closed enough. Within this tension, Said places the problem of the emergence of not only the new (or perhaps not new enough) experiments in form but also the pressures of the multitude, the claims asserted by the margin as the center fails to hold.

To the extent that modernism asserts itself as an alternative space of totality (Joyce's "encyclopedic" form, for instance), it may, as Lukács has famously argued, merely serve to obfuscate or sublimate urgent political demands.[18] Yet every such argument, intransigent as it may be in its insistence on the complicity (and oppositional divide) between the space of literature and the space of the political, must face its necessary counterpart: the possibility that modernism, by registering emergent contradictions, is, through the space of literature, giving voice to that which otherwise remains unspoken. Said's brief gloss on modernism tacitly reads it as a latter-era extension of so-called Romantic ideology. Indeed, there is a compelling argument to be made that links modernism to Romanticism's celebration of the imagination. For both, the aesthetic remains a site of possible redemption. In the case of modernism, the aesthetic imagines not only that which is yet to exist but also that which may once have existed but was never acknowledged and, within the accelerated temporality of the late modern, remains irreversibly lost to history, inaccessible to all but myth. It is in this sense that modernism takes over the syncretism of myth, or the writing of a world in which all things exist alongside each other in a kind of hyperparatactic ontology of mind (for instance, in the apparent de-realization and overcoming of any psychological "blockage" through stream of consciousness).

For Virginia Woolf, the project of writing the leftover—the problem of "what remains"—is not so easily put to rest. The figure of the remainder stands between metonym and metaphor, the part that slides into another, the one that stands in for the (absent) other. In a short prose piece entitled "The Fascination of the Pool," Woolf imagines an unfathomable depth. The story begins with a pronoun, "It may have been very deep—certainly one could not see to the bottom of it."[19] This unsounded depth figures a counter-archival site and an archival remainder onto which Woolf projects the work of the imagination and the possibility of revisiting the past through fiction.

> [The pool] held in its waters all kinds of fancies, complaints, confidences, not printed or spoken aloud, but in a liquid state, floating one on top of another, almost disembodied. . . . The charm of the pool was that thoughts had been left there by people who had gone away and without their bodies their thoughts wandered in and out freely, friendly and communicative, in the common pool.[20]

An ever-expanding liquid incompletion, the pool and its fluid boundaries resist circumscription. Scrambling oppositions between surface and depth, container and contents, outside and inside, the pool is a counter-archival repository (it "holds" what has been left behind) and a limit without discernible bounds ("certainly one could not see to the bottom of it").

A site of recollection in which what is held in common is also, despite its communicative flow, never quite shared or transparent, the pool articulates a paradoxical gathering. The drawing-together of metonymic remnant figures—voices left behind, ghostly apparitions of unrecorded lives, thoughts "not printed or spoken aloud"—its figures trace an inexhaustible return in which fragments of the past remain, available for figurative reanimation. A fantasmatic projection onto a limpid and bottomless surface, the pool also suggests that in the acts of prosopopeia through which language gives symbolic life to the dead, remembrance is always partial, incomplete, subject to revision.[21] After giving voice to several imagined fragments from the past, the story concludes, "Yet there was always something else. There was always another face, another voice."

Turned toward the flow of an unrecoverable past, Woolf's imagination invents figures through which to think what she calls, in *A Room of One's Own*, "the accumulation of unrecorded life."[22] In *Three Guineas* she calls such elusive marks of unrecording the "gap on [the] shelves."[23] The insoluble but necessary question of how to account for what the archive has failed to contain is, Woolf demonstrates, always bound up with the imagination. When the "I" of *A Room of One's Own* imagines herself speaking to the fictional Mary Beton Seton Carmichael "as if she were present," that fictive scene includes the statement, "All these infinitely obscure lives remain to be recorded."[24] What remains are spurs to the imagination, residue and returns of unrecorded life. "To read what was never written," Benjamin writes, is an echo of the oldest of mimetic desires. For Benjamin, it represents the "liquidation"—and a fragile secularization—of "magic."[25]

On (Not) Knowing

> There is an ambiguity which is the mark of the highest poetry; we cannot know exactly what it means.
>
> Virginia Woolf, "On Not Knowing Greek"

In her essay "On Not Knowing Greek," Virginia Woolf sets out by acknowledging a lack of knowledge ("For it is vain and foolish to talk of

knowing Greek"), a deficit that expands beyond any mere defect of train-
ing.[26] Rather, Woolf writes of incommensurable differences and insurmountable rifts ("between this foreign people and ourselves there is not
only difference of race and tongue but a tremendous break of tradition . . .
a chasm which the vast tide of European chatter can never succeed in
crossing"). Having said that, Woolf nonetheless goes on to write an essay
that delights in making such crossings, the bridgework elaborated out of a
writer's desire to imagine that which she cannot know.[27]

As a work of speculative "crossing," the essay addresses itself to at least
two "chasms": the "strange" motivation of the writer's desire and the unanswerable issue of its mimetic outcome. "All the more strange, then, is it
that we should wish to know Greek, try to know Greek, feel for ever drawn
back to Greek, and be for ever making up some notion of the meaning of
Greek, though from what incongruous odds and ends, with what slight
resemblance to the real meaning of Greek, who shall say?"[28] Does not this
sentence splice together, around the pivot that launches the interrogative,
some of the crucial concerns so often associated with the modern? Those
concerns include the sense of an irreparable gap between the present and
the past, a rupture that, however absolute, nonetheless requires a form of
coding, a symbolization in what might be a new form of thought; a break
from tradition that places the contemporary writer somewhere between
the cutting edge of a radically uncertain now, perhaps something like the
moment of an unanswered question ("who shall say?"), and the beginning
of a past that, the future pending, will have settled down to become, however paradoxically, a solid tradition of its own (the tradition of the new;
the canonization of the avant-garde; the institutionalization of modernism;
etc.).

As one reads "On Not Knowing Greek," it becomes clear that Woolf's
interest in "the Greeks," as well as in the abyssal divide that allows them
to "remain in a fastness of their own," has everything to do with her concerns over the present. Given that she has introduced the essay by placing
her ostensible object in the negative (as what can only "not" be known),
framing it as fundamentally beyond both translation and that form of
learning one might call fluency or perhaps a kind of reanimation (in a
sense, Woolf's point is that ancient Greek, which for her remains an inter-
nally undifferentiated category, is a dead language), it should not be surprising that the essay's desire to reinvent the Greeks has little if anything
to do with the Greeks themselves. If the essay demurs from claims of
knowledge, it does not hesitate to turn to myth, troping the Greeks as
figures of origin, of self-generating qualities and truths lost to history. "In

spite of the labour and the difficulty it is this that draws us back and back to the Greeks; the stable, the permanent, the original human being is to be found *there*."[29]

With the deictic's peculiar double gesture of simultaneously positing and pointing to a space of reference, a *"there"* held open by and inseparable from its own invocatory summons, the passage calls on a split scene of making present: *there*, collated under the sign of "the Greeks," is to be found "the stable, the permanent, the original human being," *there*, in the language of a present figuring itself through what it is not. *There*, a space of writing marked by "labour and the difficulty," a work addresses its own desire, the work of "this that draws us back and back." As *this* and *there* fold together, the text acknowledges the desire to find other such mythic, originary qualities, including, for instance, the utopian pastoral, a vision of a preindustrial, unspoiled earthly habitation. Early in the essay, Woolf notes that in trying to picture ancient Greece from the language of its poets, the contemporary imagination will begin by conjuring an English equivalent, inexact though it must necessarily be. Reading Sophocles, for instance,

> At once the mind begins to fashion itself surroundings. It makes some background, even of the most provisional sort, for Sophocles; it imagines some village, in a remote part of the country, near the sea. Even nowadays such villages are to be found in the wilder parts of England, and as we enter them we can scarcely help feeling that here, in this cluster of cottages, cut off from rail or city, are all the elements of a perfect existence.[30]

In the in-distinction between imagining the "surroundings" of Sophocles and imagining "some village," the latter transforms into an image of the premodern pastoral, an idealized, anachronistic oasis within the modern.

The trope of the utopian, rural village, with the fantasy of an unchanging world governed by commonality of tradition, ritual, and unquestioned hierarchies of power, is a staple motif of contemporary discourses of urban sociology and regionalism, where the critique of the city as corrupting, decadent, and unsustainable grows ever louder over the course of the early twentieth century.[31] Later in Woolf's essay, when the opposition between city and country, as well as between present and past, returns, Woolf sounds a note of self-consciousness, asking,

> But again (the question comes back), Are we reading Greek as it was written when we say this? . . . [Are we] reading into Greek poetry not what they have but what we lack? Does not the whole of Greece heap itself up behind every line of its literature? They admit us to a vision of the earth unravaged,

the sea unpolluted, the maturity, tried but unbroken, of mankind. Every word is reinforced by a vigour which pours out of olive-tree and temple and bodies of the young. . . . Back and back we are drawn to steep ourselves in what, perhaps, is only an image of the reality, not the reality itself, a summer's day imagined in the heart of a northern winter.[32]

Here, then, the essay reads for us the structure of its desire: To read "the Greeks," whatever they may have once been, in the present entails "reading into" them, investing their work with an imagined fullness of meaning and purity of territorial being, a kind of precastrated relationship to language, world, and earth, in other words projecting "there," in the space opened and held by their name, an ideal of untroubled humanity that Woolf finds so sorely lacking in the world of her present. And if such a projection seems to us more than a little incredible, a dubious and desperate idealization of mythic (pre)history, what does it mean that Woolf willingly acknowledges the nostalgic longing and speculative structure that drives her to invent such an ideal, to experiment in a kind of wild philology?

The punch lies in the war. Interested in the playful, embodied, shifting scene through which *The Symposium* (which she cites without naming) elaborates "truth," Woolf finds in Plato's "dramatic genius" a basis for her ongoing critique of the oppositions between philosophy and literature, the pursuit of truth and the work of the imagination. Just as, in *A Room of One's Own*, Woolf's critique of such oppositions will find a recognizably political motivation, in "On Not Knowing Greek," Woolf gives a historical texture to the essay's frame. If "the Greeks" offer the present a negative image of itself—a reverse image through which the present can see its failures, limitations, and all that it lacks—such an exercise in dis-identification takes place, Woolf writes, in a present that remains stuck, as it were, in the blind spots of its time. Without claiming to have transcended those blind spots, Woolf situates the limitations of her historical moment—that relative belatedness in which, as we have seen, the present is immobilized like a "northern winter," deprived of an originary strength and mobility associated both with maturity and youth—within a world in which the meaning of the "postwar" has yet to expire.

In the vast catastrophe of the European war our emotions had to be broken up for us, and put at an angle from us, before we could allow ourselves to feel them in poetry or fiction. The only poets who spoke to the purpose spoke in the sidelong, satiric manner of Wilfred Owen and Siegfried Sassoon. It was not possible for them to be direct without being clumsy; or to speak simply of emotion without being sentimental. But the Greeks could say, as if for the first time, "Yet being dead they have not died." They could say, "If to die nobly is the chief part of excellence, to us out of all men Fortune gave this lot; for hastening to set a crown of freedom on Greece we lie possessed of praise that grows not old." They could march straight up, with their eyes open; and thus fearlessly approached, emotions stand still and suffer themselves to be looked at.[33]

The sentence that precedes this epochalizing passage, which introduces the Greeks as "possessed" of praise bestowed in art and war, further opposes their fearless, open-eyed approach to the blocked insight of the present age. "Accustomed to look directly and largely rather than minutely and aslant, it was safe for them to step into the thick of emotions which blind and bewilder an age like our own." Woolf's characterization of her contemporary moment as incapacitated before a density of affect—the "thick of emotions which blind and bewilder"—suggests an epoch stunned by an overwhelming, uncomprehended, incomprehensible force of "emotion," an affective double bind in which what is truly felt remains to be said, at least if it is to be said "simply." Blinded and confused not only by the experience of war itself but also by an affective fallout marked by an incongruity between affect and speech, postwar literature, as Woolf renders it here, takes shape as symptom: the "sidelong" effects of an unspeakable condition, the force of feelings strong enough and sufficiently inadmissible to require the cover-ups of "sentimentality" and "clumsy" indirection.

Thus Woolf holds out the possibility for a more straightforward, less clumsy, perhaps more representative postwar aesthetic. Given that the postwar, as she characterizes it, almost instantiates a necessary but delocalized gap between the immediacy of experience and any secondary, belated aesthetic elaboration of it ("our emotions had to be broken up for us, and put at an angle from us, before we could allow ourselves to feel them in poetry or fiction"), the notion of what might constitute a representative response grows less clear. Where does the preparatory work of deferral— that of the breaking up and angling that is required ("before we could allow . . .")—take place, and has it indeed taken place? Precisely insofar as Woolf's argument here remains uncertain, the essay writes itself within the horizon of the postwar, a period defined less by its distance from or comprehending glance back at the war than through its own "clumsy" attempts to distinguish itself from the confusion of an age. The essay's conclusion returns us to the stakes of separating confusion from something else. Woolf's investment in the Greeks remains an issue of turning away from—perhaps overcoming, escaping, or compensating for—the (over-?) compensatory, and for Woolf altogether inadequate, false "consolations" of her own age.

> There is a sadness at the back of life which [the Greeks] do not attempt to mitigate. Entirely aware of their own standing in the shadow, and yet alive to every tremor and gleam of existence, there they endure, and it is to the Greeks that we turn when we are sick of the vagueness, of the confusion, of the Christianity and its consolations, of our own age.[34]

*   *   *

Yes, I was thinking, we live without a future. That's what's queer.

Virginia Woolf, *The Shorter Diary*

> Things can't go on for ever, she thought. Things pass, things change, she thought, looking up at the ceiling. And where are we going? Where? Where? . . . The moths were dashing round the ceiling; the book slipped on to the floor.

Virginia Woolf, *The Years*

If, as many recent critics have argued, Woolf's *To the Lighthouse*, even with its markedly perspectival form and foregrounding of "thought" as the privileged domain of actuality and event, does not, as Lukács has argued of modernism, amount to a "denial of history," how does the novel engage with the demand, perhaps an impossible one, for literature to address, whatever such an address might entail, the vexed relationships between war and aesthetics, the effects of historical catastrophe on the language and experience of literature?[35] And if the novel's middle part, "Time Passes," so often ignored in criticism on the novel (Auerbach skips it almost entirely), can be read as a writing of the war, of war as an experience of language, the question remains: How does the text, with its fragmented lyricism, temporal compression, and drift toward the cosmic, register and give form to those vast, wide-ranging, and complex set of events summed up by the blunt category heading of "the war"?

In "The Ideology of Modernism," Lukács excoriates modernism for reifying a world that lacks meaning and offers no normative grounds for politics. Modernism's overemphasis on form is coincident with a "lack of hierarchic structure," or any hierarchy of values from which to launch a meaningful critique of capitalist ideology. Modernism's ennobling of a general "flight into psychopathology," Lukács argues, is, after 1914, exacerbated into "an all-pervading obsession," by which he seems to imply an overinvestment in the figure of the neurotic, even as the war proliferates the "normality" of the pathological. For Lukács, rather than representing an investment in the historical and social conditions of the war, such an "obsession" can only mean a failure of the aesthetic to provide any synthetic, objective point of view, a failure that appears as a mere turning away from the world, a "negation of outward reality." Thus modernism participates in an aesthetic overvaluation of psychopathological experience, such that "man is reduced to a sequence of unrelated experimental fragments; he is as inexplicable to others as to himself." Modernism, Lukács concludes, "leads straight to a glorification of the abnormal and to an undisguised anti-humanism."[36]

What interests me in Lukács's essay is that it offers, in exaggerated form, an unapologetic version of some of the more common arguments launched against the modernist experiment. Modernism, synthetic and antisynthetic, is criticized for being both overly totalizing and altogether fragmented. It turns out that the word "modernism," like "realism," as Fredric Jameson has argued, can be put to a great many uses.[37] Perhaps every generation reinvents a modernism of its own.

Particularly given Woolf's repeated interrogations of the locations of "reality" ("But, I ask myself, what is reality? And who are the judges of reality?"),[38] the issue of war in her texts—the writing of the reality of war; the writing of war as reality—requires us to resist the notion that we know what "the war" looks like, that we question whether and how we know what signifies war. Similarly, in her ongoing critique of the framing of history, or that fleeting and skittish totality Woolf sometimes calls "life," or reality in its dominant, traditionally masculine forms of appearance, Woolf repeatedly calls for a shift in the field, away from the presumptive conventions of the "big" or commonly recognized event, toward a newly refined, less easily validated attunement to the possibility of the "small," introducing something like an aesthetics of the molecular and infinite, a neutral approach to the psychic-oblique, an attempt to record without prejudice the "atoms" of the mind.[39]

In her critical writings, Woolf fiercely rejected definitions that would demand of literature, in the pronominal ontology rejected by Mrs. Dalloway, that it fulfill an abstract ideal, as if literature "were this or were that."[40] Yet, in many of her essays, as she puts forward a critique of her contemporaries (tethered under the pejorative title "the materialists," with the most frequently named representatives H. G. Wells, Galsworthy, and Arnold Bennett), Woolf offers a sketch of the priorities and challenges that, as one of her essay titles puts it, "strike" her as confronting modern

literature. The problem with contemporary literature, Woolf argues, begins with the fact that it does not, at least not yet, exist, not as such, not
as a recognized body or critically agreed-upon set of works. In "the chaos
of contemporary literature," no one critic, no "centralizing influence," has
managed to dominate the discussion. "There is no name which dominates
the rest. There is no master in whose workshop the young are proud to
serve apprentice."[41] As she entertains the masculinist fiction according to
which, "Once upon a time, we must believe, there was a rule, a discipline,
which controlled the great republic of readers in a way which is now unknown," Woolf makes mention of a related problematic, in which the lack
of a leading critical voice is juxtaposed with an observation about the difficulty of sizing up the exceedingly complex "currents" of the "modern
world." In a rhetoric that figures the present as liquid and various, Woolf
writes of an unbounded, or "scattered," culture of complexity, conjuring
the surfeit of change, flux, and information so often associated with modernity's dual, contradictory movements: the dizzying, splintering forces
of fragmentation, constant upheaval, and agitating uncertainty alongside
an ever-increasing vortex of generalized chaos, a logic of structural compulsion and tendential uniformity in which, despite the vanishing grounds
of definitive, stable hierarchies of judgment, it remains possible to speak
of the "world" as one. "The scattered dinner-tables of the modern world,
the chase and eddy of the various currents which compose the society of
our time, could only be dominated by a giant of fabulous dimensions. And
where is even the very tall man whom we have the right to expect?"

Woolf's image of a representative, prosaic scattering invokes the problematic of the modernist sublime: Faced with the "too-much-ness" of an
everyday world in which details spill over, failing to add up to a vision or
whole, the subject may be overwhelmed or underwhelmed, but in either
case the "chase and eddy of the various currents" stops short of giving
over to any figure of exceptional height, the triumphant verticality so often
associated with the sublime at the brink of vastness and the void. Or, as
Woolf describes the effect of reading contemporary prose, "The flash is
soon over, and there remains with us a profound sense of dissatisfaction.
The irritation is as acute as the pleasure was intense."[42]

"Time Passes" is perhaps best known for the abrupt, bracketed death of
the novel's central character, Mrs. Ramsay, who dies, "rather suddenly,"
in a subordinate clause. Thus the event of her death is itself an empty
space held together by multiple gestures of enframing: Mr. Ramsay's arms,

themselves twice "stretched out" in a repetition divided by, and rhetorically inclusive of, Mrs. Ramsay's death, create a syntactic structure and visual image in which the extended arms articulate a space of longing and loss, a gesture of holding (nearly an embrace) that outlines desire in the absence of its object; typographically the brackets function like Mr. Ramsay's arms: framing a void in space.

The writing of a space on the precipice of a void recurs throughout "Time Passes." The representation of Mrs. Ramsay's death dramatically enacts the acuteness of loss, and the rest of "Time Passes" projects the possibility and problem of loss on a larger scale. I focus on two figures from this part of the novel: "certain airs" and a certain "feather." Together, they portray an allegory of war that is ominous in scale yet without clarity of end or meaning.

The subject and agent of vision in "Time Passes" is a figure, "certain airs," as in the following passage, in which the lyricism of the section, its abstraction and profusion of an elemental chaos, turns to darkness.

> So with the lamps all put out, the moon sunk, and a thin rain drumming on the roof a downpouring of immense darkness began. Nothing, it seemed, could survive the flood, the profusion of darkness which creeping in at keyholes and crevices, stole round window blinds, came into bedrooms, swallowed up here a jug and basin, there a bowl of red and yellow dahlias, there the sharp edges and firm bulk of a chest of drawers. Not only was furniture confounded; there was scarcely anything left of body or mind by which one could say, "This is he" or "This is she." Sometimes a hand was raised as if to clutch something or ward off something, or somebody groaned, or somebody laughed aloud as if sharing a joke with nothingness. (125–126)

Darkness, downpour, flood—figures of a general and vast catastrophe, a shift so total it abides only a speculative positing ("as if") of an exchange with "nothingness." As the "profusion of darkness" invades the space of the house, the dependence on such speculation will continue, often in the mode of "as if," as if to suggest that the narrator's access to reality has been blocked. Deprived of its own stealthlike vision and capacity to see through "keyholes and crevices" (the movement of so-called free indirect discourse, the ability to "go round the table unveiling each of these people, and their thoughts and their feelings, without effort like a light stealing under water," as the narrator gives Mrs. Ramsay to think as if of herself [106]), the text shifts gears, no longer drifting from the external (the world "outside" a character's mind, for instance; or the exterior of a house) to the internal (what takes place in and as the language of thought; the other side of an architectural threshold, the inside of a house) with such seamlessness as to problematize such boundaries altogether. Whereas the vision of the narrator was, in the novel's first part, not so much omniscient as telepathic, able to cross, penetrate, and scramble lines of communication, in "Time Passes," the narrator is held back, kept at a step of remove. Its vehicle of transport and vision is what it calls "certain airs."

These "airs," evident in the following passage, are a double figure, tracing a tension between blindness and insight, vision blocked and revealing. They are, in the language of the previous passage, what comes "creeping in," a figure of thought crossing the barriers of darkness and the "blinds." As such, they are also more and other to the narrator's vision. They require the work of imagination, which itself can only stretch toward but not reach around the invisible agent of vision. "Almost one might imagine them." The "airs," a privative figure for what can and must be imagined in the absence of insight. Not unlike Andrew's parable of his father's work—he tells Lily, in a quick pedagogy of reduction, "'Think of a kitchen table then,' he told her, 'when you're not there'" (23)—the figure of the airs allegorizes the problem of thinking the object without a subject, the thought-thing as if without the mediation of the thinker.

> Nothing stirred in the drawing-room or in the dining-room or on the staircase. Only through the rusty hinges and swollen sea-moistened woodwork certain airs, detached from the body of the wind (the house was ramshackle after all) crept round corners and ventured indoors. Almost one might imagine them, as they entered the drawing-room questioning and wondering, toying with the flap of hanging wall-paper, asking, would it hang much longer, when would it fall? Then smoothly brushing the walls, they passed on musingly as if asking the red and yellow roses on the wall-paper whether they would fade, and questioning (gently, for there was time at their disposal) the torn letters in the waste-paper basket, the flowers, the books, all of which were now open to them and asking, Were they allies? Were they enemies? How long would they endure? (126)

The syntax here disturbs, in multiple ways, our ability to identify a single, coherent agent of action. The very first phrase, "Nothing stirred," introduces a condition of generalized stasis, an interior space filled out only in the negative, through a creeping void that suggests the hollow, eerie melancholy of abandonment: a house without life, a general condition of uprooting and disorder, a habitation on the verge of falling (as might the wallpaper) into an abyss of some kind—perhaps merely succumbing to that seemingly benign form of loss called "fading." From the "nothing" of the first sentence, the passage moves (like the "airs," language moves—even and especially where "nothing stirred"), introducing the movement of imagination and language, the rhetoric of the question.

Critics have not failed to note the passage's allusion to a wartime idiom of "allies" and "enemies," a rhetoric of division that cannot but echo the Great War's legacy of an all-encompassing militarism.[43] The anachronism of such an echo is interesting for reading the time of "Time Passes," which, as the textual corridor that links "The Window" and "The Lighthouse," can be read as an unexpected relocation of the interstice of the "interwar." Typically associated with the period between the First and Second World Wars, the interwar becomes such only with and from the point of view of the latter's occurrence. Without positing a logic of inevitability or teleological unfolding that would take for granted what remains in the future, we can read the novel as an interwar novel precisely in its anticipatory return to the scene of an anxious, proleptic coding of the possibility of looking back on the Great War, or to the writing of the time of war as it strides toward an imminent and uncertain future. In other words, the novel helps us rethink the periodizing frame imposed by the "interwar," approaching it not simply as a finite, backward-looking interval emergent only after the fact (after the beginning of the Second World War, the "interwar" designates a terminal history between the end of one war and the start of another), but as a turbulent effect of writing the story of the unsettled experience and unfinished ends of the Great War.

Certainly, in terms of historical chronology, *To the Lighthouse* comes after the war. Not only by virtue of its date of publication, but through a framing of events in which the war, however obliquely and without clarity of reason, comes to an end, the novel bears the traces of issuing from and onto a postwar present. By the end of "Time Passes" and the beginning of "The Lighthouse," the novel's third and final part, the war has come to some kind of end. Like the cleanup of the house whose abandonment allegorizes the ambivalence and "too-much-ness" of the war and its aftermath, the end of the war is not much of a finishing. It is in this sense—as a questioning of what it means for an era to be present (or not) to itself, as a critique of the postwar period as if it knew how to look back upon the war, to put the past behind it and see itself as if in the clear—that Woolf's text challenges us to rethink the notion of the interwar novel.[44]

In terms of diegetic narrative time, "Time Passes" anticipates the coming of total war, an inundation of "darkness" that has already begun its work, threatening to topple what remains of the domestic and political order of the past. At the same time, the outcome of the scene of abandonment represented in the above-cited passage, along with any answers to its many questions ("questioning and wondering, toying with the flap of hanging wall-paper, asking, would it hang much longer, when would it fall? . . . asking, Were they allies? Were they enemies? How long would they endure?") remains uncertain. In a later passage, the "stray airs" return, figured through apposition as the "advance guards of great armies" (128–29), a mixed rhetoric of anachronism that suggests a directed, resolved temporality of battle, the neat choreography of the old-fashioned campaign. If such notions of "greatness" appear, in retrospect, as the obsolete fantasies of a naive, prewar (or rather pre-postwar) ideology, the text questions the desire to locate and contain the war as past.[45]

"Time Passes" reflects upon the projections of a hopeful, messianic imagination and the providential theodicy for which, in spite of a proliferating "emptiness," a meaningful peace will, in the end, have redeemed the losses and costs of war. Over and over again, the novel returns to the swelling takeover of the "stray airs," lending to them the air of an apocalyptic threat.

> So with the house empty and the doors locked and the mattresses rolled round, those stray airs, advance guards of great armies, blustered in, brushed bare boards, nibbled and fanned, met nothing in bedroom or drawing room that wholly resisted them but only hangings that flapped, wood that creaked, the bare legs of tables, saucepans and china already furred, tarnished, cracked. What people had shed and left—a pair of shoes, a shooting cap, some faded skirts and coats in wardrobes—those alone kept the human shape and in the emptiness indicated how once they were filled and animated; how once the looking-glass had held a face; had held a world hollowed out in which a figure turned, a hand flashed, the door opened, in came children rushing and tumbling; and went out again. Now, day after day, light turned, like a flower reflected in water, its sharp image on the wall opposite. Only the shadows of the trees, flourishing in the wind, made obeisance on the wall, and for a moment darkened the pool in which light reflected itself; or birds, flying, made a soft spot flutter slowly across the bedroom floor. (129)

What was once full and animated remains, now, only as trace. As the passage continues, where one might expect an accent of decrepitude, Woolf returns to an aesthetic of enduring "loveliness" and "stillness," as if to suggest that the absence of life has brought an end to the discontinuities and ruptures of ending, the final forms of a world in an unchanging scene, a still life.

> So loveliness reigned and stillness, and together made the shape of loveliness itself, a form from which life had parted; solitary like a pool at evening, far distant, seen from a train window, vanishing so quickly that the pool, pale in the evening, is scarcely robbed of its solitude, though once seen. Loveliness and stillness clasped hands in the bedroom, and among the shrouded jugs and sheeted chairs even the prying of the wind, and the soft nose of the clammy sea airs, rubbing, snuffing, iterating and reiterating their questions—"Will you fade? Will you perish?"—scarcely disturbed the peace, the indifference, the air of pure integrity, as if the question they asked scarcely needed that they should answer: we remain. (129)

The irony of the survivor's lament: In lieu of a sentimentality of a mournful peace, Woolf represents a house in which what remains does so only in the form of a peace textured by "indifference, the air of pure integrity." Such as it is, the coming of peace exacts its own form of violence: an "integrity" whose purity is achieved by washing its hands of the bloodbath of the war.

Indeed, as "peace descended," and the figure of the toiling Mrs. McNab returns "as directed to open all windows, and dust the bedrooms" (130), the novel interrupts linear temporality to return to the tension between wartime and its aftermath, the time of war and the time of peace. Mrs. McNab, classed figure of human agency restored (and for some critics the laboring force whose restorative efforts, a kind of humanity in the "last instance," represent the ambivalence of Woolf's elitism), gives Woolf's narrator occasion to introduce a workaday melancholy. For Mrs. McNab, "something . . . was robbed of meaning" (130). She herself embodies the contradictions of realizing the loss, for "she was witless, she knew it" (130).

Yet there is a leaning toward goodness, the desire of "the hopeful."

> As summer neared, as the evenings lengthened, there came to the wakeful, the hopeful, walking the beach, stirring the pool, imaginations of the strangest kind—of flesh turned to atoms which drove before the wind, of stars flashing in their hearts, of cliff, sea, cloud, and sky brought purposeful together to assemble outwardly the scattered parts of the vision within. In those mirrors, the minds of men, in those pools of uneasy water, in which clouds for ever turn and shadows form, dreams persisted, and it was impossible to resist the strange intimation which every gull, flower, tree, man and woman, and the white earth itself seemed to declare (but if questioned at once to withdraw) that good triumphs, happiness prevails, order rules; or to resist the extraordinary stimulus to range hither and thither in search of

some absolute good, some crystal of intensity, remote from the known
pleasures and familiar virtues, something alien to the processes of domestic
life, single, hard, bright, like a diamond in the sand, which would render
the possessor secure. (132)

No such security is to be had, not as object or possession. As fantasy and
narrative of the triumph of the good, of civilization, of the desire for progress, perhaps. But Woolf returns to a faint murmur—not a strident exhor-
tation but a writing of the event—that renders peace meaningful only as a
fantasy, a story in which the postwar constitutes progress made and insight
gained. For Woolf, such a narrative is so uncompelling that the events of
"The Lighthouse," the third part of the text, suggest no such difference
at all. For some, this may be too easy a solution, suggesting that, among
others, Andrew Ramsay's death remains suppressed or too insignificant.[46]
For Woolf, it is a way of writing the postwar as after-the-war but not as
goodness restored or insight gained. At stake in this uncertainty is the
projection of retrospective meaning, the prolepsis of ends and reasons as-
cribed to the war, the narrative and interpretive framing of the war as if
after its end. Throughout the unfolding of "Time Passes," Woolf scrambles linear temporality, fathoming and frustrating an anticipatory imaginary for which destruction must have—will have had—logic and limits. In
the following passage, which appears just after the questions "Were they
allies, Were they enemies? How long would they endure?", Woolf pushes
the fiction of conclusiveness in its dual directions: a desperate, if persistent,
desire to hold the present as ground, to contain the uncertainty of the
future, and in particular to resist an onslaught of death and disappearance;
the futility of such any such hope, which, were its desire to be achieved,
would come as the immortality of death.

Unreason, confusion, and inhumanity threaten to take over altogether
in the seventh section of "Time Passes," as time is jumbled into a "gigantic chaos." The scale becomes cosmic and inhuman.

So some random light directing them with its pale footfall upon stair and
mat, from some uncovered star, or wandering ship, or the Lighthouse even,
the little airs mounted the staircase and nosed round bedroom doors. But
here surely, they must cease. Whatever else may perish and disappear, what
lies here is steadfast. Here one might say to those sliding lights, those fumbling airs that breathe and bend over the bed itself, here you can neither
touch nor destroy. Upon which, wearily, ghostlily, as if they had feather-
light fingers and the light persistency of feathers, they would look, once,
on the shut eyes, and the loosely clasping fingers, and fold their garments

wearily and disappear. And so, nosing, rubbing, they went to the window on the staircase, to the servants' bedrooms, to the boxes in the attics; descending, blanched the apples on the dining-room table, fumbled the petals of roses, tried the picture on the easel, brushed the mat and blew a little sand along the floor. At length, desisting, all ceased together, gathered together, all sighed together; all together gave off an aimless gust of lamentation to which some door in the kitchen replied; swung wide; admitted nothing; and slammed to. (126–127)

Starting with the "random light" and then in the figure of a collective yet ineffectual, indeterminately meaningful sigh ("an aimless gust of lamentation"), the passage tropes the "airs" as placeholder-name for an imaginary addressee invested with the power of keeping death at bay ("Here one might say to those sliding lights, those fumbling airs that breathe and bend over the bed itself, here you can neither touch nor destroy"). The image of the "feather," seemingly redundant to the weightlessness of the "airs," will reappear later in "Time Passes," as a figure of the questionable logic and weight of history.

Section 7 offers the novel's most brutal writing of the war, a world tumbling on the verge of a void. Conspicuously lacking any human subject or spectator (or, in tune with the passage's initial auditory accent, "any one to listen"), the section moves between figures of earthly and cosmic chaos, a poetics of "tumbling and tossing" and "battling and tumbling," building up a figurative universe spliced together through figures of violent, meaningless repetition.

Night after night, summer and winter, the torment of storms, the arrow-like stillness of fine weather, held their court without interference. Listening (had there been any one to listen) from the upper rooms of the empty house only gigantic chaos streaked with lightning could have been heard tumbling and tossing, as the winds and waves disported themselves like the amorphous bulks of leviathans whose brows are pierced by no light of reason, and mounted one on top of another, and lunged and plunged in the darkness or the daylight (for night and day, month and year ran shapelessly together) in idiot games, until it seemed as if the universe were battling and tumbling, in brute confusion and wanton lust aimlessly by itself. (134–35)

As Woolf's passage runs together figures of chaos and inundation, it too "tumbles," creating a sense that the narrative is hastened and threatened by the very "confusion" of the scene it represents. In what remains of his treatise on the sublime, Longinus (or, for preference, pseudo-Longinus) includes asyndeton as one of sublimity's exemplary figures. In asyndeton, "the words tumble out without connection, in a kind of stream, almost getting ahead of the speaker. . . . Disconnected and yet hurried phrases convey the impression of an agitation which both obstructs the reader and drives him on."[47] Similarly, Woolf's passage, pivoting on the figure of the "amorphous bulks of leviathans whose brows are pierced by no light of reason," hovers on the brink of blurred sight and descent into darkness, agitated but not overcome by the "idiot games" it so piercingly introduces.

Yet what does it mean to say that Woolf's passage effects such sublimity? To suggest a sublimity of style, a "greatness" of form alone, is inimical to the discourse of the sublime, which tends to point to a zone "beyond" or to that something "more" that makes the sublime not only a moving target but the effect of an aim, a desire to uphold if not elevate meaning. If for Longinus, "something higher than human is sought in literature," and if "sublimity raises us towards the spiritual greatness of god,"[48] then the question in reading Woolf becomes the elevation not of terror conquered but of violence exposed in its sheer stupidity. It is also the "aestheticization" of war; the accusation of aesthetics as a crime, as Adorno has argued, is, on its own, a meaningless critique. That Woolf turns to the language of sublimity and beauty to engage with the violence of the war does not mean that she merely ignores the war or cleanly displaces ("sublimates") violence into art. The experience of this section of the novel is an experience of the world at the perch of an abyss. For Woolf, that abyss includes a measure of beauty—if seen only in their absence, by the figurative vision and imagined gaze of the airs—but it is a "terrible" beauty, devoid of the more pedagogically merciful, wish-sustaining, regressive sentiments of any Arnoldian goodness, the taste for sweetness and light.

The second paragraph of section 7 reads:

> In spring the garden urns, casually filled with wind-blown plants, were gay as ever. Violets came and daffodils. But the stillness and the brightness of the day were as strange as the chaos and tumult of night, with the trees standing there, and the flowers standing there, looking before them, looking up, yet beholding nothing, eyeless, and so terrible. (135)

Section 9 takes us once again to the edge. At the end of the preceding section, as an exhausted Mrs. McNab turns away from the house, she desists before an excess of disorder and the demand it imposes on her, both of which have become "too much." There is a banality in this excess, the prosaic life of a woman left to do work that is more than she can bear.

> She sighed; there was too much work for one woman. She wagged her head this side and that. This had been the nursery. Why, it was all damp in here;

the plaster was falling. Whatever did they want to hang a beast's skull there? gone mouldy too. And rats in all the attics. The rain came in. But they never sent; never came. Some of the locks had gone, so the doors banged. She didn't like to be up here at dusk alone neither. It was too much for one woman, too much, too much. She creaked, she moaned. She banged the door. She turned the key in the lock, and left the house alone, shut up, locked. (137)

Returning to the house as figure for a world pitched to sink, finally and forever, "downwards to the depths of darkness" (138), the section begins with a scene coursing with figures of abandonment and overflow, a mixed rhetoric that outlines the inertial decay of the house through the fecundity of an indifferent nature.

The house was left; the house was deserted. It was left like a shell on a sandhill to fill with dry salt grains now that life had left it. The long night seemed to have set in; the trifling airs, nibbling, the clammy breaths, fumbling, seemed to have triumphed. The saucepan had rusted and the mat decayed. Toads had nosed their way in. Idly, aimlessly, the swaying shawl swung to and fro. A thistle thrust itself between the tiles in the larder. The swallows nested in the drawing-room; the floor was strewn with straw; the plaster fell in shovelfuls; rafters were laid bare; rats carried off this and that to gnaw behind the wainscots. Tortoise-shell butterflies burst from the chrysalis and pattered their life out on the window-pane. Poppies sowed themselves among the dahlias; the lawn waved with long grass; giant artichokes towered among roses; a fringed carnation flowered among the cabbages; while the gentle tapping of a weed at the window had become, on winters' nights, a drumming from sturdy trees and thorned briars which made the whole room green in summer.

What power could now prevent the fertility, the insensibility of nature? (137–38)

The imposition of the language of nature suggests what might be called a naturalization of violence, a reduction or commensuration of the war to the "insensibility of nature." At the same time, such figures resist logic, making nature in excess of reason or understanding: on the other side of the mirror.

It will be a "feather" on which the chance of peace depends. The feather, the utterly meaningless, aleatory, purely empty contingency of chance. A feather, a clinamen, a figure of movement beyond prediction and the inertia of this world.

For now had come that moment, that hesitation when dawn trembles and night pauses, when if a feather alight in the scale it will be weighed down.

One feather, and the house, sinking, falling, would have turned and pitched downwards to the depths of darkness. In the ruined room, picnickers would have lit their kettles; lovers sought shelter there, lying on the bare boards; and the shepherd stored his dinner on the bricks, and the tramp slept with his coat round him to ward off the cold. Then the roof would have fallen; briars and hemlocks would have blotted out path, step and window; would have grown, unequally but lustily over the mound, until some trespasser, losing his way, could have told only by a red-hot poker among the nettles, or a scrap of china in the hemlock, that here once some one had lived; there had been a house.

If the feather had fallen, if it had tipped the scale downwards, the whole house would have plunged to the depths to lie upon the sands of oblivion. But there was a force working; something not highly conscious; something that leered, something that lurched; something not inspired to go about its work with dignified ritual or solemn chanting. Mrs McNab groaned; Mrs Bast creaked. They were old; they were stiff; their legs ached. They came. . . . (138–39)

The emphatic turn of the "but." The apocalyptic introduced and thwarted. The moment of a "now" stalled before apocalypse, an all-falling either-or that turns on nothing but a "feather." All but for a feather.

CHAPTER 3

Walter Benjamin on Radio:
Catastrophe for Children

The name of the philosopher who took his life while fleeing Hitler's
executions has, in the more than twenty years since then, acquired a
certain nimbus, despite the esoteric character of his early writings
and the fragmentary nature of his later ones. The fascination of the
person and of his work allowed no alternative other than that of
magnetic attraction or horrified rejection. Everything which fell
under the scrutiny of his words was transformed, as though it had
become radioactive.

THEODOR ADORNO, *Prisms*

Preface: "under the sign of suicide"

Virginia Woolf and Walter Benjamin may have in common more than the
fact that both ended their lives in the peculiar, and inevitably disturbing,
death-event called suicide.[1] As essayists and readers, both resist the lure
of mastery, producing works that take pleasure in the accumulation and
deepening of recursive thought. Woolf refuses almost every form of alle-
giance, and while Benjamin vacillates between calls of affiliation (marxism,
Jewish theology, messianism, Zionism, the bonds of kinship and friendship), his identification with and understanding of the demands of any
one structure, cause, or system remain uneasy and ambivalent. Defined in
negative alignment, both remain curiously open for, and productive of, a
wide range of passionate attachments. Frequently cast as "icons," both
figures have attained a status of exemplarity that has proven remarkably
versatile in its redistribution of the meaning attributed to the authorial
name. And then, too, there is the widely reproduced image of the face.[2]
Perhaps most of all, the two have become figures of the author beloved.

We might speculate that the spectacular, and spectacularly agitating,
scenes of authorial death have played no small part in sustaining the critical longing and melancholic identification that surround the two figures.

71

If suicide demands explanation (none of which can ever satisfy, as the question is not only "why"—why did she do it, why did he not wait—but "why
not"—why not earlier, why not later, why wait, why remain, why not I),
it also opens onto a fantasy of "unnecessary" and "avoidable" death. Such
fantasmatic insistence (perhaps, as Blanchot and Žižek might suggest, a
denial of an act that wants to deny and defy death)[3] sustains the possibility
of a supplementary immortality, an alternate universe in which the (still)
living writer would have left us with more. More to read, more to work
with. If only she had not done what she did, if only the war had not placed
him in such circumstances. If only Leonard had been more vigilant (or
less so), if only Adorno had come through in time.

Needless to say, it is only because Woolf and Benjamin have left us,
suicidal leave-taking notwithstanding, with an already considerable body
of work that such desire for more presents itself. Abetted by the notion of
untimely death, as well as a narrative of life "incompleted," the longing
for a different outcome in death (as nondeath, deferral of death, sovereignty over death) redoubles the alluring fictions of authorial presence:
symbolic immortality as the animating, auratic, singular voice that endures, a force of life and creative expression in excess of embodied being
and materiality of the trace.

Transmissions of the Voice Interrupted

In Benjamin's case, the fantasy of extended life finds a renewed outlet in an
audiophilic detour. Widely associated with his writings on photography,
Benjamin is less well known for his contributions to the early history of
radio. Between 1927 to 1933, Benjamin made more than eighty broadcasts
over the new medium, working at stations in Berlin and Frankfurt. Some
of these performances were given in the form of *Hörmodelle* (listening
models, or radio models); some were commissioned specifically for Berlin
radio's *Jugendstunde* or the *Stunde der Jugend* on Südwestdeutschen Rund-
funks in Frankfurt.[4] In either instance, perhaps all the more so for the
latter given the directed specificity of its target audience, the issue of
programming—of culture *as* (pre)programmed—asserts some force and
sway. In the extant manuscripts of his radio addresses, including those
performed for children, Benjamin can hardly be said to presume a definition of his addressee ("children") or to reify the figures of receiver, audience, public. (Indeed, it is part of Benjamin's hope for radio that it might

create, as a medium of mass address and appeal, a generative and self-critical dialectic of the popular, both as form and collective ideal.)⁵ In approaching Benjamin's radio works for children, I am reminded of a comment Benjamin makes in the context of his critique of children's literature: "If there is any field in the whole world where specialization is bound to fail, it must be in creating things for children."⁶

Benjamin's disparagement of his radio works can hardly account for the relative scarcity of critical attention given to the material. If it is thanks to Gershom Scholem that we are aware of Benjamin's reference to "some piddling radio matters" and that we can cite Benjamin as having discounted his radio lectures as being "of no interest except in economic terms," it is also Scholem who reminds us, "This denigratory assessment of WB's radio work . . . must be interpreted in the context of his negative attitude toward much of the work he did for money. Yet most of these texts also contain sediments of his decidedly original way of seeing."⁷

As an apparatus controlled by capital and the state, radio emits, for Benjamin, an ambivalent modernity.⁸ Benjamin's radio programs figure an interrupted, broken transmission, in part because their archival residuum remains incomplete. At the same time, such incompletion, beyond any carry-over of the author's biographically contingent narrative, represents a problem structurally endemic to any history of the audio universe: as event, object, and medium, sound takes place by a dispersal that is subject to fading. "As historical object, sound cannot furnish a good story or consistent cast of characters nor can it validate any ersatz notions of progress or generational maturity. The history is scattered, fleeting and highly mediated—it is as poor an object in any respect as sound itself."⁹ If the print archive (including the archives of recorded sound), as site of collection, retention, and storage for the future, is also a zone of oblivion, an off-site dumping ground for memory and thus for forgetting, the fleeting materiality of the sound event calls attention to the difficulty of sustaining the fiction (whether paranoid, idealized, or Foucauldian-empiricist) of the archive as enregistered totality contravening any leakage or loss. For every act of recorded perception, whether inscribed as photographic or audio reproduction, a further act of validation and reinscription is necessary, and to the extent that such iterability remains both pending and possible, no final oversight or programmatic overhearing has ever taken place, not that we can speak of.

Without claiming for the sound event the status of the uniquely live experience (a distinction rendered all the more paradoxical for being dependent on the technologies of inscription that would record, if not invent

it as such), how to think about the archival inexistence of the author's
(posthumously available) voice, and more important, about the desire in-
stantiated around this figure of the void?[10] Associated with a fleeting syn-
chronicity of reception, an event of dissemination expanded (both spatially
and catachrestically) in the figure of "broadcasting," the radio performance as live but unrecorded event introduces something of a primal, one-
way audio telegraphy, a disappeared scene of originary emergence to
which we have access only in secondary forms.[11] Recast as the scene of a
medium in its infancy, the early years of radio are, perhaps, especially
freighted with the paradoxes and burdens of transmitting loss; whether as
fragile yet materially extant forms from the prehistory of sound recording
(species of "incunabula," those remnants of early recording technologies
that are notoriously "difficult to hear"), or in the more abstract form of the
inexistent remainder (recordings that were not—were not made, cannot be
found, can be heard only as that which cannot be heard at all), broadcasts
from the early years of radio reach us, to the extent that they reach us at
all, as halting installations, fragments stalled on the way. Stops along the
path of development, they are also fugitives, escapees, and spurs to structures of preservation and narratives of capture.[12]

The spectral death of the author returns to us in our longing for the
signature tone of the voice. As Eduardo Cadava has argued, "Death,
corpse, decay, ruin, history, mourning, memory, photography—these are
the words that Benjamin has left for us to learn to read." Fundamentally
resistant to any fantasy of the harmonious whole, the corpus as if reani-
mated and restored in full, these words, left to us by Benjamin but precisely noncoincident with any sustaining origin, "correspond to the
cremation of his work, a cremation in which the form of the work—its
suicidal character—reaches its most brilliant illumination, immolated in
the flame of his own criticism."[13] To Cadava's collection of Benjaminian
words, we might now add a few others: radio and audiography in the absence of the voice. The radio typescripts, another Benjaminian grave.

Catastrophe without End

The fascination of danger is at the bottom of all great passions. There is
no fullness in pleasure unless the precipice is near. It is the mingling of
terror with delight that intoxicates. And what more terrifying than
gambling?

                                        Walter Benjamin, *The Arcades Project*

Reading the writing of the age of catastrophe, how can we not return to Benjamin's prose image of the "angel of history," the prose of thought at an impasse: a reading of historical progress that can fantasize the possibility of divine redemption but for which, in the absence of any such break, can only, as if such repetition were inevitable, return to a mechanistic logic in which history is governed by an external yet immanent limit, an underived force of power whose figure is that of a "storm."

> Where we perceive a chain of events, [the angel] sees one single catastrophe which keeps piling wreckage upon wreckage and hurls it in front of his feet. The angel would like to stay, awaken the dead, and make whole what has been smashed. But a storm is blowing from Paradise; it has got caught in his wings with such violence that the angel can no longer close them. This storm irresistibly propels him into the future to which his back is turned, while the pile of debris before him grows skyward. This storm is what we call progress.[14]

The image of a storm that blows from the direction of Paradise suggests an otherworldly yet operative power, a force over which neither the human nor the angel has control; the image's paradoxical "directionality," in which the blow comes from Paradise yet drives the angel toward the future, suggests that the storm is an effect of an originary propulsion, an overpowering urgency from which we are cut off yet to which we are fully and blindly subjected; where the angel's "face is turned toward the past,"[15] we are stuck in that past, bits and pieces of the catastrophe that pile up endlessly from the ground. Yet mortal subjection does not exclude symbolic and visual investiture, and it is with an ambivalent, indexical nod toward such investiture—"This storm is what we call progress"—that the thesis asserts its rhetorical force. What does it mean to say that "this storm," a figure of illegible desire and violence (the divine? the paternal?), is for us, called by us? "What we call progress," the storm is other to yet also an effect of our mixed-up desire and language, our insistence on calling on "progress"—as a word, perhaps as an idea, an image, a wish. Calling on and calling attention to an act of nominative persistence—"Das, was wir den Fortschritt nennen, ist dieser Sturm [This storm is what we call progress]"[16]—the passage registers complicity with, and yet takes distance from, the vision and habit of the "we," the collective whose view of progress it enables us to see and perhaps to think again. Neither dismissed as mere myth nor negated as tendential mistake, "progress" is first of all the act of returning to—keeping faith with?—the urge and appeal held in a word.

In its repetition, Benjamin's Thesis IX has become something of an allegorical image for the twentieth century as dialectical impasse. Its central problematic is that of the place and nonplace of the catastrophic event from the point of view of the future—including that view of the future "we call progress." The angel of history is a figure of the singular witness who *might* gather from the mounting debris, from the scattered signifier and the symbolic in ruins, a new and newly possible account of the past. The passage suggests that such an account would not reproduce the usual view of history as "a chain of events," the normative, terrestrial vision of history as a succession of the inevitable and irreversible. Perhaps the angel, in his more-than-mortal vantage point, might restore to the past a redemptive and restorative wholeness—if only. If only there were such an angel, if only he could do as he pleased, if only "to stay, awaken the dead, and make whole what has been smashed." This phrase (rephrased, perhaps, in the tone of a child, one for whom wanting and succor are all) expresses the ambivalence of the passage as it turns the possibility offered by the image of the angel into an impossible, unrealized, even altogether wrecked ideal.[17] The angel can see the wreckage, he figures the very possibility of seeing as superhuman anamorphosis, but his vision is impotent given the force of another catastrophe, the storm of what we call progress.

It might seem that the passage offers a sacrificial view of the catastrophe: Although the angel can see the all of the horror in front of him—the dead, the fragments of an ideal—he cannot see what is behind him, the force of a future toward which he is compelled. If the passage hints at the triangulations of the dialectic—catastrophe, or history seen from above but suspended and left behind; the desire for redemption, wholeness, uplift negated; the future as more of the same—it is as if its animating force, situated somewhere between the "we" that calls and the "storm" (mis)recognized as "progress," has yet to make its move. Perhaps, the passage allows, the wish of "if only" will survive to return in the future, as a different future, as more than so much dead weight. Perhaps, in the words of Scholem's poem, cited by Benjamin as epigraph, the possibility for a different scene of the angel's messianic revision hinges on an issue of fortune, something like a turn of "luck."[18]

If the "angel of history" is Benjamin's most famous prose image, some of its appeal is the way in which it condenses, critically and without didacticism, the difficult, unresolved relation between history-as-catastrophe and history-as-progress, a tension that inheres within the twentieth century as it questions the ongoing failure of Europe's Enlightenment narrative and ideals. Similarly, the image of the angel's gaze as it stares out upon an ever-mounting verticality of destruction, the "hurled" totality of history's ruins, invites us to rethink our understanding of the image and meaning of "catastrophe." Here, the gesture of the "hurl" problematizes the notions of stasis, fixity, propinquity, or continuity suggested by the phrase, "one single catastrophe." Rather, it is as if catastrophe, both subject and object of the "hurl," arrives from a distance, and not only once, but over and over again. To land "in front of his feet," the accumulated wreckage must somehow, even as it seems to remain at his feet and stand just beneath him, cross a threshold from below or afar. Though it is "one single catastrophe," its assertive violence is divided and takes place as more than one event: Gathering and cumulative, catastrophe piles "wreckage upon wreckage," and at the same time, expulsive, catastrophe "hurls."

Benjamin's image of catastrophe thus raises questions about catastrophe's temporality: Rather than catastrophe as ultimate ending, final expenditure, the last turn in an unredeemed earthly chronicity, catastrophe goes on and on—and on. Indeed, it is in the nonarrival of the "last" of catastrophe that Benjamin's image points to one of the century's related critiques of catastrophe-as-eschaton or revelation. Remindful of Beckett's idiom of the permanent penultimate, the impossibility of finishing, Benjamin suggests the catastrophe of iterative, inexhaustible exhaustion, the catastrophe of ending-without-end.

With such issues in mind, I turn to a different scene of a Benjaminian writing on catastrophe. The texts to which I refer have, curiously, received a lack of critical attention; as widely disseminated as is Thesis IX, these texts remain, remarkably, on the margins of Benjaminian scholarship. The site of an incomplete audio file, these are the texts, or rather what remains of them, of Benjamin's radio addresses. In particular, I focus on two texts produced under the auspices of his participation in radio programs for children.

Catastrophe for Children

In February and March 1932, Walter Benjamin gave a radio broadcast on the recent history of technology, or, as he put it, the forward-moving history of "technological advances."[19] Broadly, his subject in "The Railway Disaster at the Firth of Tay" is the emergence in the nineteenth century of new technologies of building and transport, or those "constructions that had no precedent in the past" (564). In particular, Benjamin focuses on the railway, as well as on structures that, making use of iron in building, introduced new architectural forms such as the "first exhibition palaces . . . the first covered markets, and above all the first train stations" (564). Opposing such "firsts" and their moment of emergence to the contemporary understanding of technology, Benjamin appears to build a narrative of reception history that would begin in nonknowledge and proceed, with a conspicuously naive hopefulness (not even in his most explicit messianism is Benjamin so insistent on a progressive history), to arrive with confidence in a present that has mastered technology as object of knowledge: "When people first attempted to smelt iron and build steam engines at the beginning of the nineteenth century, that was a very different matter from what happens today when scientists and engineers go about developing a new airplane or even a space rocket or some other new machine. Today we know what technology is" (563).

With its emphatic optimism, Benjamin's statement, "Today we know what technology is," strikes a curious charm. It is a rather delightful, indeed altogether fanciful, suggestion, the underlying stakes and seriousness of which could not possibly have been lost on Benjamin, for whom the question of technology, including that of radio, tends to raise the specter of war. As he later argues, in the essay for which he is perhaps best known, any discussion of contemporary technology cannot avoid the politics of aesthetic pleasure, especially when it comes to the spectacle of death.[20] Here, as if keeping fright at bay, anticipating a charge of a merely gratuitous use of shock, Benjamin plays down any errant, undue interest in the spectacle of horror. With a finely tuned pedagogical pitch (elsewhere Benjamin addresses the pedagogical, and critical, potential of radio as a new medium, a technology whose history begins with the contemporary generation),[21] Benjamin sets out to tell a story, a kind of fairy-tale, in which the note of victory is to be doubly triumphant.

Benjamin builds his narrative on a railway disaster, the collapse, on December 28, 1879, of the Tay bridge in Scotland.

> I am going to tell you today about a railway disaster. Not so much to recount a horrifying story, but rather to put the event in the context of the history of technology and more particularly of railway construction. A bridge plays a role in this story. The bridge collapsed. This was without doubt a catastrophe for the two hundred people who lost their lives, for their relatives, and for many others. Nevertheless, I wish to portray this disaster as no more than a minor episode in a great struggle from which human beings have emerged victorious and shall remain victorious unless they themselves destroy the work of their own hands once more. (563)[22]

Benjamin will go on to recount the "story" of the building of the bridge, which was completed in May 1878, and of the collapse only a year and a half later. The conclusion of the story is a triumphant embrace of technology in its transition from "infancy" to maturity, the latter represented by the 1889 construction of the Eiffel Tower, "a monument to engineering calculation" (567). Having juxtaposed the failure of the Tay bridge in 1879 and the successful erection of the Eiffel Tower a decade later, Benjamin wants to lend support to the difference between them by arguing that the latter "acquired a meaning" when it eventually gained the functional capacity of supporting radio telegraphy (567). Still, his conclusion hardly serves to prioritize the value of function. Instead, Benjamin wants to elevate the tower symbolically, holding it up as a monument to the power of engineering and its techno-extensions of "thought."

> Eiffel and his engineers had built the tower in seventeen months. Every rivet-hole had been precisely positioned in the workshops to within a tenth of a millimeter. Each of the twelve thousand metal fittings, each of the two and a half million rivets, had been machined to the millimeter. There was no sound of chisels on the work site; in the open air as much as in the builders' workshops, thought reigned over sheer muscle power, which it was able to transmit via cranes and secure scaffolding. (567)[23]

In the representation of such transmission, Benjamin abstracts the place and power of technology, figuring its triumph as the seamless, superhuman extension of the mind of the engineer. Drawing on the carrying power and transmitting effect of the signifier, the passage tunes into the silence of the work site, troping the negative to tell the story of an aesthetic-historic leap: from the sound era of the chisel to the hermetic thought reign of the engineer. Spanning this difference is the hinge figure of the chisel, its sound summoned in retreat. Just as the "sound of chisels" is displaced off-site into the image of a remote past, so too is "sheer muscle power" withdrawn from the scene. Fetish image of the pretechnological within technology, the brute force of the laboring body functions as dialectical fastener, linking present ideal (the perfectly engineered mechanism and the towering, filigreed object that it "thinks" into being) with a certain uncontrolled remainder, the vanishing but not altogether controlled threat of disruption and disorder. Whether as surplus or lack of force, too much brute energy or its insufficient precision, the staying power of "sheer muscle power" works, like a misfit or mislaid rivet, to undermine and offset the object's symbolic standing, the reassuring conclusion of the tower's having "acquired a meaning." Hovering in exclusion, the negated remainder—"sheer muscle power," or the brute force of the laboring body; the possibility of the tower's not "having" or "transmitting" a certainty of meaning—forebodes the unvanquished threat of collapse.

Fossilized as prehistory, the substratum of force is spatially, temporally, and telegraphically dislocated into the congealed form of so many "rivets," the unit of standardized mechanicity that upholds the tower as symbolic monument and vertical platform, the signal-site for modernity's new powers of transmission: the wireless or telegraphic dissemination of "thought" into the world. (The contemporary notion of telepathy, familiar terrain to popular and scientific culture by 1932, would redouble the achievement of wireless telegraphy: If the latter sends language as data over radio frequency, the former would transmit thought without language over frequencies unknown).[24] Bypassing muscle power, the engineer transmits thought, Benjamin suggests, as if by thinking alone. Thus "thought reigned." As for the supporting roles of "cranes and secure scaffolding," Benjamin's image gives them a status somewhere between mental prosthesis (an extension of the engineer's mental plan) and frequency (as in the manner of radio transmission, where the voice travels, as it were, over the invisible "lines" of the airwaves). Securing control over the technological in the figure of a prime thinker—the mind of the engineer—Benjamin's idealist image raises the question of the programming and automation of thought, or the writing of the mind as representative exception to the technological. Above all, whatever supports it may use (cranes, secure scaffolding, other machines, the bodies of other men, rivets, language, gravity, etc.), the engineer's mind, as Benjamin imagines its towering achievement, becomes a figure of a self-governing and accident-proof operating system.

The fantasy written in Benjamin's concluding remarks can be read according to the figure of the rivet. The rivet fastens, holds, joins. The riveting thought keeps the listener engrossed. The rivet, perfectly machined, serves as a flawless device for pinning together, locking adjoining parts, canceling the void. Benjamin's desire (in retrospect, a desperate one) is riveted to the idea that the history of technology will not repeat the destructive horrors of the past, that, unlike the train over the Firth of Tay, the struggle between human beings (perhaps between humans and nature, in any case a struggle to be addressed below, as the names of its opponents are not altogether clear) will not end with a mere plunge "into the void" (566). Similarly, the hope is that Benjamin's words, along with their somewhat encrypted trajectory, will not dissipate before making their point, their audience, their destination. As a radio address, Benjamin is speaking to that newly formed mass, the general listening public, sending out a message, in the form of a lengthy parable, about the possible futures of technology. Having given an exemplum of the historical potential for catastrophic pitfalls, Benjamin wants to suggest that such disasters, whether construed as accidents or mistakes, are now in the past, summoned only to reassure the present of a superior technological fate.

It is difficult to conceive that the writer who will produce the "Theses on the Philosophy of History," including the famous prose image of the angel of history, has voiced such a reassuring story of technology's meaningful history and fortunate future. Only two years previously, Benjamin published a different story. In "Theories of German Fascism," Benjamin sounds one of the century's prominent notes, that of the problematic asymmetry between, on the one hand, the buildup, often called advances, in technologies of destruction, with their increasingly explosive power and range of force, and, on the other, the relative nonadvancement in any field of human affairs, whether social, ethical, or political, that might keep the former in check. (It is on this note that Freud, for instance, will end *Civilization and Its Discontents*, turning the rhetoric of "total war" to its unhappily logical conclusion, "Men have gained control over the forces of nature to such an extent that with their help they would have no difficulty in exterminating one another to the last man.")[25] Benjamin, emphasizing the gap between recent material developments in technology and any accompanying "moral illumination" that would effect any control over their future use, writes, "one might say that the harshest, most disastrous aspects of imperialist war are in part the result of the gaping discrepancy between the gigantic means of technology and the minuscule moral illumination it affords."[26] The problematic of technology and the future of warfare is a preoccupation of the interwar period. Benjamin's concern is not only with the possibility of a repetition of the last war, but also with the escalation in violence that will represent, when next war comes again, the triumph of fascism.[27]

The expository preface of "The Railway Disaster at the Firth of Tay" presents a more equivocal, less salutary knowledge of technology. The remarks introduce a note of warning and caution, an accent that is entirely absent from the rest of the address. We recall that Benjamin advances that he is going to tell a story about a train wreck, not "so much to recount a horrifying story, but rather to put the event in the context of the history of technology and more particularly of railway construction." In other words, the narrative interests him, as far as he wants to acknowledge, not for the mere spectacle of horror, but for its edifying place within a larger history. (Such a gesture of denegation is also part of the century's anxious preoccupation with the value, or lack thereof, in the writing of disaster and the aesthetics of catastrophe. Against the charge of a gratuitous, vulgar, or otherwise insufficiently purposeful act of representing the "horrifying" event, art and philosophy will find it necessary, if also impossible, to justify any attempt to give voice or narrative form to the event. More specifically, Benjamin's prefatory comment here articulates a mounting concern, particularly pronounced after the First World War, over exhibiting any enjoyment in the representation or consumption of horror as spectacle.)

Benjamin positions his interest as an issue of reading a certain struggle. I cite the passage again.

> A bridge plays a role in this story. The bridge collapsed. This was without doubt a catastrophe for the two hundred people who lost their lives, for their relatives, and for many others. Nevertheless, I wish to portray this disaster as no more than a minor episode in a great struggle from which human beings have emerged victorious and shall remain victorious unless they themselves destroy the work of their own hands once more. (563)

It is in this moment that Benjamin historicizes the struggle between the human and technology. Though the stated focus of the address remains the contextualization of the disaster in Scotland in 1879 within a progressive narrative of human mastery over technology, and therein to imply a mastery over the threat that such a disaster might happen again, here the struggle is not so much a question of greater knowledge or advances in engineering or the duality between technology and the forces collectively called "natural." (As Benjamin explains, the cause of the Tay bridge collapse, though a matter of dispute, was by all accounts related to a storm.)[28] Rather, the struggle concerns the very question of the political present and the history of technology. The clause of exception, written in the phrase that begins "unless," textures the essay, in an oblique yet unmistakable way, as a commentary on the present as "interwar" in the sense that it looks back upon the horror of the First World War, and the monstrous events during which "human beings . . . destroy[ed] the work of their own hands," and at the same time anticipates the possibility of such destruction happening "once more." The bridge disaster, as the talk's apparent subject, is simply not available for transcription into the phrase or for substitution as its referent; although Benjamin's reading of the disaster does suggest an interpretation whereby the collapse is read, retrospectively and in the light of later knowledge, as an effect of human error, or as an episode in the history of mismanagement and malfeasance, the emphasis on the Tay bridge event as a "minor episode" places the focus elsewhere.

The "major" narrative Benjamin addresses shifts from a struggle between engineering and nature, or between superior and inferior technological knowledge, to a different, less abstracted scene and history of battle.

The notion of the bridge disaster as a representative moment or minor episode in a larger victory becomes, like the reference Benjamin will make to the illustrations of Grandville, an anachronistic pleasantry, an optimism whose naive delight in technology becomes a parody of the "playful dimension" Benjamin reads in the early appearance of iron architecture. Of Grandville's satirical illustrations in *Un Autre Monde*, published in 1844, Benjamin returns, here as well as elsewhere, to a particular image among the text's many "jokes and fanciful stories" (564). Benjamin describes, in an ekphratic translation from visual to verbal image, Grandville's anthropomorphic, Paris- and bourgeois-centric, representation of the planetary cosmos, where the famous ring around Saturn becomes "nothing other than a balcony running entirely around the planet and on which the inhabitants of Saturn strolled in the evening to get a breath of fresh air" (564). Illuminated by gas lighting, a bridge connects Saturn to the other planets of the cosmos, in a mock figuration of the compression of space through the iron-constructed ways of the rail and the bridge, projects of horizontal engineering and distance spanning that, not unlike the space of the book, carry the promise of transport. Yet as an image of a space apart, an elsewhere of mind and cosmos, the Saturn in Grandville's narrative is quite distinctly not otherworldly. The planetary other world opened for travel in the text and images of *Un Autre Monde* is, as Benjamin points out, no more "exotic" than the exoticism for sale and display on earth.

Grandville's satire takes aim at the industrialization and commodification of the world, including the worlds of myth, which are rendered exotic because obsolete in modernity. In a part of the passage to which Benjamin refers but leaves out of his excerpted citation, Grandville has his main character run into the figure of Charon, formerly the ferryman to the underworld, now unemployed, as he has been "ruined by the construction of a bridge of iron over the river Styx." Thus Saturn becomes a forced retreat within the total world of capitalism for its refugees and rejects.[29]

Walking on the bridge, as if on his way from one planet to another, is an imp, a figure of the upstart, solitary, smoking flaneur, through whose gaze the illustration focalizes the sight of Saturn's ring as a balcony. Filled with tiny figures of the multitude at leisure, the ring is a space of the domesticated exterior, a place that, like the partially enclosed zone of the arcades as Benjamin reads their historical moment, allegorizes a threshold of modernity, the spread of the "cult of the commodity."[30] For Benjamin, the playful appropriation of technology in Grandville's imagery represents the "enthronement of the commodity, with its glitter of distractions."

The transformation of the world, including its cosmological forms of appearance, into familiar scenes of such enthronement is, Benjamin argues,

> the secret theme of Grandville's art. Whence the split between its utopian and cynical elements in his work. The subtle artifices with which it represents inanimate objects correspond to what Marx calls the "theological niceties" of the commodity. The concrete expression of this is clearly found in the *spécialité*—a category of goods which appears at this time in the luxuries industry. World exhibitions construct a universe of *specialties*. The fantasies of Grandville achieve the same thing. They modernize the universe. In his work, the ring of Saturn becomes a cast-iron balcony on which the inhabitants of Saturn take the evening air. By the same token, at world exhibitions, a balcony of cast-iron would represent the ring of Saturn, and people who venture out on it would find themselves carried away in a phantasmagoria where they seem to have been transformed into inhabitants of Saturn.[31]

In Grandville, Benjamin finds a world on the threshold of complete normalization, that is to say the reification, of industrial capitalism. By calling attention to the ambivalence between the "utopian" and "cynical" interpretations of that world as represented in Grandville's imagery, Benjamin suggests the "dialectic at a standstill," or a moment of historical change in which the eventual "outcome," as seen from a later period, is caught between the unknown and the inevitable. In such an image of historical development, the naive interpretation of the new is not a symptom of mere blindness or false consciousness. After describing Grandville's image, Benjamin asks his audience, "Do you see what I mean when I said that, at the time, people did not really know how they should react to technological advances? The latter were not without a comic side in their eyes" (564). Making an implicit connection between Grandville's moment and his own, Benjamin suggests, in what can appear now only as a preposterous provocation, an unknowingness as to the coming future in the history of technology. It is as if the only way to tear such a history out of the governing demands of imperialism and capitalism, and along with them the drive toward war, is to take flight into the negative fantasy of revolution by force of natural disaster, the fiction of an inhuman power strong and other enough to escape and divert the disastrous repetition of human history.

Benjamin delivered "The Mississippi Flood of 1927" on March 23, 1932. Perhaps Benjamin's most sustained reflection on the politics and culture of the United States, the text tells a condensed narrative organized around another scene of horrific catastrophe, the failure of the Mississippi River levee system during the 1927 flood. Like "The Railway Disaster," it is a story of frightful horrors, blocked paths, and death in numbers. And like "The Railway Disaster" (and like many of Benjamin's other radio scripts), it follows a three-part structure: introduction to the event, context, and relevant history; reading from an eyewitness account or a survivor's story, or, if no such text is available, reference to an artifact associated with the event; concluding remarks in which Benjamin makes links between the previous sections and a related issue in the present.

As Benjamin's account emphasizes, the story of the flood is saturated with a history of politics and power. The horrors that emerge out of the Great Flood of 1927 are all the more horrifying for Benjamin as effects of political failure and racial injustice. As a "natural disaster," the event is not a narrative of engineering overcome by nature, embankment technology failing before the awesome, insurmountable might of a river. For Benjamin the central conflict is rather the "horrific and miserable events" occasioned by a politically protected act of violence, a sacrifice demanded at gunpoint by one class from another. It becomes, Benjamin says, the story of a "bitter civil war." Its most glaring moment of contradiction is the political decision, enforced by armed troops and maintained through a "state of siege" (effectively martial law), to prevent the inundation of the city of New Orleans by blowing up the levees of its neighbors.

Benjamin's story of the flood opens with a description of the "line" of the river as read from a map. His language conjures a visual image only to turn to the problem of sight deceived.

> When you open a map of middle America and have a look at the Mississippi, a gigantic 5000 km-long river, you'll see a bold and somewhat curvy line, filled with turns, but heading rather clearly from North to South, a line on which you could surely depend, if you were so in need, like on a boulevard, or on a railroad line. The people, however, who live on the banks of this river, the farmers, the fishermen and even the city folk, know that this appearance is deceptive. The Mississippi is in continuous movement, and not only its volumes of water moving from its source to its mouth, but also its banks, which are constantly altering themselves.[32]

If the Mississippi is a force of untamed and unpredictable currents (Benjamin later refers to the "restlessness and unreliability" of the river's path), its elemental powers of movement, surge, and self-alteration have long since been altered by the work of an elaborate system of redirection and containment. The system of embankments or levees (or rather, not so much a system as a piecemeal aggregate) built on its banks, Benjamin states,

> protected the land that lay behind them but only at the expense of those neighbors who stood to suffer even more. It was in this way that most of the lower-lying plantations gradually protected themselves. . . . Now you will surely be able to imagine what it must have meant to these planters, who owned nothing but their land, when one day it was required that they tear down the embankments with their own hands and expose their plantations to the destructive violence [*zerstörenden Gewalt*] of the water. But this is precisely what once happened and now I will tell you about this most horrific and miserable [*schrecklichsten und trostlosesten*] of events, the great flood of 1927.

Benjamin relates the story of the militia assembled to resist the forced destruction (by explosives, not by hand) of the levees sacrificed to save New Orleans, a story that turns into a history of repetition,

> the onset of a bitter civil war that only increased the horrors of the natural catastrophe [*die Schrecken der Naturkatastrophe*]. The farmers whose land was to be sacrificed in order to save the capital were among the poorest in the country. . . . Thousands of farmers were resolved to fight rather than to pay for saving the city with the destruction of their own fields. . . . But the government would not allow itself to be intimidated and proceeded with the demolition. New Orleans was saved but 100,000 square miles of land was under water. The number of those made homeless in the region reached half a million.

After recounting a brief history of the levee system and its massive scale ("These constructions rank among the biggest state projects in American history"), Benjamin tells the story of three brothers who refused to evacuate their home, eventually finding themselves without egress. "Before they knew it the path [*der Weg*] leading them was blocked by a mighty spit of water: they were cut off and would remain so. Only one of the three would escape with his life." It is this surviving brother's first-person account that Benjamin includes.

What Benjamin does not mention is the structure of racist violence that was inscribed in the events of the flood.[33] However, the concluding remarks of Benjamin's address provide a peculiar and pointed redirection of that violence.

So much for the raging elements of the Mississippi. But some other occasion we'll have a look around its banks at a time when the river flowed peacefully in its bed; but by no means has it always been peaceful. For a long time now I've planned to tell you the story of America's greatest and most dangerous secret society, compared to which all bands of whiskey smugglers and criminal gangs are child's play: the story of the Ku-Klux-Klan. Once again we will find ourselves on the banks of the Mississippi, but this time facing the raging element of human cruelty and violence. And the dams that the law has built to contain them have held up no better than the actual ones made from earth and stone. And so, stay tuned for the Ku-Klux-Klan and Judge Lynch and other unsavory characters that the human wilderness of the Mississippi has given us, and continues to give us to this day.

The address of "The Mississippi Flood" relates its horrors without any uplifting outcome. Benjamin's address takes up the structuring tropes of a contemporary discourse of racial engineering that figures white mastery as a failing system of flood control, a dialectic of the civilizing mission fighting to hold back a "rising tide of color."[34] The racialized naturalization of the threat of nature, as Benjamin argues, is the bridge that links the dialectic of Enlightenment to the fantasy of racial purity.

Generations of Catastrophe

In a reading of "The Railway Disaster at the Firth of Tay," Emily Apter has found a "signal text of planetary comparatism," a term Apter uses to stake out the possibilities and challenges of a new, non-Eurocentric (yet also nonhomogenizing or easily globalized) comparative literature.[35] Benjamin's text, Apter argues, "leads us from the baseline of small disasters (accidents) to an end-point of mass destruction."[36] Such a trajectory, woven into Apter's larger discussion of the history and future of comparative literary studies, finds in Benjamin's text the undecidable, perhaps promising, relay between "catastrophism" and "planetary comparatism" ("catastrophism begets a planetary comparatism—or perhaps follows logically from it").[37] If catastrophism threatens to result in the "end-point of mass destruction," in Apter's argument it also conjures the abyss in which the "untranslatable," or the radical alterity embedded within every language, becomes an alibi for Anglo-European ignorance. Catastrophism augurs the dead end, albeit a potentially explosive one, in which the possibility of any encounter with alterity is buried, killed, destroyed. Something like the end-point implied in Benjamin's allusion to the threat of a repetition of world war (to say "planetary" war seems to miss the point, as the idiom of the planetary is reserved, in its critical, quasi-utopian register, for a different, perhaps historically unprecedented translation of the terms of collectivity and the writing of belonging), catastrophism carries no guarantee of "begetting" a new "planetary comparatism," as the point—of Benjamin's text as I read it, and I believe of Apter's essay as well—is precisely that the future, whether as the next iteration of catastrophe or as the retroping and changing institutionalizations of the necessary impossibility of translation—*might* also "translate" as a site of and name for alterity.

To elucidate this point, one should note that Apter's argument draws on Gayatri Chakravorty Spivak's elaboration of the "planet" as figure in a critical rewriting of the system-logic of globalization. "The planet," Spivak argues, "is in the species of alterity, belonging to another system; and yet we inhabit it, on loan." At the same time, a simple substitutive opposition or reversal of terms will not do. "It [the planet] is not really amenable to a neat contrast with the globe. I cannot say 'the planet, on the other hand.' When I invoke the planet, I think of the effort required to figure the (im)possibility of this underived intuition."[38] The planet is a figure of and name for thinking radical alterity, along with the necessary impossibility of translating "it" along the way: it, the (writing of the) planet; it, the radically other, a figure of the world we inhabit that "remains underived from us."[39] In another context, speaking of "Earth," Spivak has noted that the planet, is "singular and irreplaceable." Along with whatever the planet as earth may "give"—whether understood as ground, nature, resource, habitat, ecoform, or other taxonomic derivation; such a list, in its rough terminality and incompletion, should remind us of the unresolved problems of writing earth or, as Spivak puts it, the "inexhaustible taxonomy of names"[40]—the problematic of the substrate, or what Marx theorized as the production of surplus in "primitive accumulation," returns in the postcolonial present in the attempt to capture and classify the terrain of "biodiversity," or the translation of "life" in all its species forms (perhaps, in the end, there will only have been one, the supergenre of the genome) into the codes of science and capital. We are—or so we might hope—still learning to read Benjamin's broad(re)casting of the future of anything so grave as the "minor catastrophe."

CHAPTER 4

On the Late Sublime: W. G. Sebald's
The Rings of Saturn

Fidelity, the virtue of the poet, is faithfulness to something that has
been lost. It imposes detachment from the possibility that what has
been lost can be grasped here and now.

THEODOR ADORNO, *Notes to Literature*

Archive for Aliens

In the late 1970s, when the National Aeronautics and Space Administration launched the twin *Voyager* space vehicles, the interplanetary mission carried a truly far-out, indefinitely addressed *envoi*. Aboard each probe was an object called a Golden Record, a name appropriately resonant with the project's quasi-Frazerian cosmo-anthropological syncretism and presumably as unintentional as the implied relays between magic, kitsch, and science. What is this so-named object? After seeing its image, one might be tempted to say that the phrase is literal enough: Flat, circular, and gold, the object looks something like the LPs of the time.[1] Yet, even understood as audio-phonic medium (in this case the plate is neither vinyl nor gold, but copper) on which music is stored and made available for repeated play ("recorded"), the meaning of a "record" quickly proves opaque. This is not merely to say that the literal, as usual, breaks down (it does), nor is it to suggest that the record's absurd fantasy, the desire of its creators and participants that it should, one day in whatever universe and for any other, be received as a comprehensible and representative document, is all that exceptional. Its celebratory exhibition of a collective, specular ego-ideal recalls the museo-archival humanism of 1955's "The Family of Man," Edward Steichen's much-criticized universe in the image, whose fantasy of encapsulating the totality of "man" in the object and medium of the still photograph is its terrestrial precursor.[2] (As for the Golden Record's extra-terrestrial address, the idea of the alien is a figure for the all-knowing other, the one who will, in receiving the message, have understood us better than we understood ourselves.)[3] At stake, or on board if you like, is the very question of mediatization, of what it means for a thing to carry, collect, preserve, transport, represent, legitimate a set of signifiers as rep-resentative—of a past and previously recorded event, perhaps including by concealing the nonevent of editing, or, in this case, representative of a collective totality, the curated, posthumous archive of humanity.

Among the sounds and images recorded for the posterity of the species, sent to the great big Other for deep storage and eternal homage to a civili-zation anticipating its own extinction, no photograph of corpses heaped together like so much skeletal excrement was admitted. Such an image, by contrast, does appear in W. G. Sebald's *The Rings of Saturn*, where the *Voyager* spacecraft appears in connection with a chain of associations linked by historical and archival displacement, a variegated and oblique movement from one trace of reading or site of recollection to another.[4] Earlier in the day, the narrator takes shelter in the Sailors' Reading Room in Southwold, a "kind of maritime museum" (92) where he happens upon a certain book. *Happens upon*: A sense of the unplanned, unintended, per-haps unmotivated encounter is crucial to the novel's strange mixture of outsetting and inertia, movement in abeyance of destination or arrival, a wandering path traced only in the negativity of vanishing forms of pres-ence. As peregrination or pilgrimage, the narrator's journey on the coast of Suffolk maintains a peculiar tension between insistence and refusal: At-tracted to the shifting, thin margins of edges, shoals, and shorelines, as well as to sites of destruction and decay, the novel's landscapes are not quite divisible into the picturesque and its well-framed scenes. Tending toward variations on the expanding void, presentations of thought glued to a limit that is itself subject to doubling and dispersal, while refusing to make such forms of the "negative" mere obstacles to be overcome, steps along the way toward a better world, the text makes its construction of a reader's itinerary a kind of sublime offering, imposing what Nancy calls the "suspension of art" at stake in the sublime.[5]

The End of Sublimity?

As a critical concept, the sublime has hit something of a wall. It is none too popular these days, not that it has ever been all that comfortable with commonality of appeal. The fragility of its distinction has long depended on and done battle with at least two opposing fronts: The alternative line of the beautiful, with its Kantian appeal to harmony in judgment, wages against the questionable ethics of an aesthetic bent on pain, on the sublime as it takes pleasure in surviving sacrifice and enjoying the limit-idea of the sheer vastness of the void, the unimaginable engulfment of total annihilation. And then there is the threshold below—the fall into the ridiculous—the basement of failure, the surfeit that comes to nothing, the inevitable mis-"step" that keeps the sublime on its toes, always just on the verge of falling flat.

Much has been written lately on the exhaustion of the sublime. Often with reference to Adorno's comments on the problem of the aesthetic "after Auschwitz," critics have questioned the consumption of mass death as an aestheticized spectacle, with the implications of taking too much pleasure or having the wrong kind of enjoyment in gazing a bit too comfortably on the suffering of others, unable to grasp the reality of that suffering in full.[6] If we recognize that Adorno's critique does not add up to a condemnation of art or representation as such, the important question is not how to avoid aestheticization but how, if at all, the aesthetic might register, or fail to register, in its form and language, the unprecedented barbarity and horror of the event. If Adorno's critique remains dialectically invested in the problem of the aesthetic (in, for instance, his reading of Beckett), it is as if the provocative ban on representation implied in his remarks has been displaced onto Lyotard, who stands accused of heralding the repetitious sublimity of the postmodern and the limitations of knowledge.[7]

One of the critiques of the sublime after Auschwitz emerges out of the contradiction between the sight of images of horror and the idea that such images should produce the questionable gain of merely telling us, over and over again, that we cannot do more than present the limitations of representation, or "the unpresentable within presentation itself."[8] Owing to Lyotard or no, debates surrounding the contemporary sublime have had to confront the question of whether and in what sense sublimity, whose life-affirming encounter with the terrorizing and terrifying has traditionally required some measure of distance from any actuality of presence or excessive proximity with the sublime object, can be said to take place "now." The now of the event, which converges with the difficult temporality of trauma and the irruptive experiences of terror, violence, and the wholly unanticipated, raises questions about the continued investment in one of modernity's earlier poetics of the formless, the unassimilated, and the new: the aesthetics of shock. As is suggested in Benjamin's

writings on Baudelaire, the twentieth century takes from the late nineteenth (along with a more distinctively Romantic aesthetics, including the
inherited tradition of the natural sublime, from the century's early decades) an interest in the problem of art and the "massifying" formations,
or unstable antiformations, of urban life. The growth of the nineteenth-
century metropolis, increasingly textured by the dual forces of densifica-
tion (more people, more noise, more of less) and fragmentation (the difficulty of producing a coherent topography and visualization of the social
field in the mode of hypostatized urban landscape), produces a discourse
in which the fantasmatic blast of sublimity shifts: Without going so far as
to say that the awesome forces of nature, as in Kant's dynamic sublime,
are entirely left behind (indeed, they may return in new forms, transvalued
under the sign of scarcity and the threat of disappearance), one can say
that the contradictory effects of capitalism, empire, and industrialization
bring into play new forms for the mind's confrontation with the work and
appearance of the limit: the limits of the human, a category that unfolds
into others, the limits of power, thought, imagination, reason, representation, language, survival.

In many of its traditional, for the most part eighteenth-century accounts, the sublime presents a story of some form of gainful victory at and
over such limits. Confronted with an infinite expanse, vastness, or object
of unthinkable magnitude, the mind experiences reason's triumph over the
imagination's inabilities—its inability to grasp the whole, to frame its object as one, to hold itself and its sense of itself together before a (nearly)
overwhelming threat. Related to sensory shock, an experience of an object
or force of overwhelming magnitude (a magnitude which, for Kant, borders on the infinite, and whose very formulation can be put only negatively: *"That is sublime in comparison with which everything else is small"*)
introduces the related threats of psychic disintegration and the vertigi-
nous.[9] Where for Kant the gain is an issue of reason's ascension, Edmund
Burke, for instance, will return to an empiricism of the sensory apparatus,
such that the sublime, as physical-psychical experience, offers a "rush," a
forced opening for pleasure by way of the threat of pain—"for pleasure
must be stolen."[10]

And even into the twentieth century, the sublime maintains a relationship to being just near enough to the edge of an abyss (the bottomless
ocean, the vertigo effect of peering over the top of any protective barrier,
the sight of the technological in its incomprehensibility) that its signature
frisson and fantasy lives on: the combination of pleasure at the felt threat
of pain; the experience of an enjoyment in (more) than survival; the fantasy

of getting just close enough to danger that (the fantasy of) almost not making it out alive is a thrill. Yet, for reasons including those mentioned above, the stock of the sublime has been perforated, perhaps displaced by the onrush of terrifying historical events and their multiplying representations, perhaps annulled by them altogether. One line of argument suggests that the sublime has withdrawn from sheerness of power and greatness of height into dullness of the ever-level and the remorselessly flat; from energizing encounter into a thickness of boredom, disaffection, indifference, or impotence (the gendering of the sublime as masculine is a staple of the discourse); from the rarified into the merely banal. Through mass culture and widespread screens of access to the image, a kind of normalization of terror's image (we recall Sontag's argument that the dissemination of terror as image or spectacle has made the shocking banal), the "more" of the unexpected, or the excess of the extreme, has been rendered altogether less so; now, by default of context and the commodification of any and every possible experience, the sublime always now stands to verge on kitsch. In a culture of fright-on-demand and TV-safari, the very idea of the sublime can appear far too precious indeed; a gesture toward the might of nature or nature-in-surfeit can produce the sigh of stuffy air, coming off as merely quaint, antiquated, or even just plain cute.

Yet "cute" can also be a word for an offense; the culture of "lightness" and even the discourse of impotence cannot be reduced to a historicizing mechanicity of affect, or even explained by a critique of the commodity fetish, without also raising questions about sublimity and the twentieth century's other histories in which violence, altogether too real, alternatively erupts into reality and, precisely in relation to our (non)desire to grasp and consume its afterimage, recedes into a museo-archival background: In the background of the consuming normalization of the extreme experience by a culture of commodified entertainment (from Benjamin's reading of the Universal Exhibitions to today's products of extreme sports, roller coasters, horror films, virtual reality, and the war game) are the related histories of the industrialization of genocide and the commodification of memory.[11] When Virginia Woolf writes of uncertainty in judging the "greatness" of the contemporary work of art, she refuses to allow for the market as the decisive space in value's calculation.[12] That critical suspension—perhaps a distinctively modernist affirmation of a different logic of aesthetic judgment—may now appear a utopian, anachronistic gesture. As Hans Magnus Enzensberger argued in 1958, the critique of tourism is inescapably internal to the discourse of tourism.[13] Similarly, there is no critique of the museum outside of the proliferating culture of the blockbuster exhibition. It is in this context—that of late capitalism and the many iterations of the obsolescence of the avant-garde—that Slavoj Žižek's reading of the problem of the contemporary sublime appears noteworthy.[14]

My purpose here is not to rehabilitate the sublime but instead to return to its vocabulary to read the space of writing and difference elaborated in Sebald's novel.

If the voluminous criticism that surrounds Sebald's work has already come to constitute something like a field (whether one calls it "Sebald studies" or, in a disparagement whose phrasing has grown cold, the "Sebald industry"), its emergence has been remarkable for its speed and intensity; a mere twenty years ago, not a single one of the works that have become the object of such feverish scholarly attention and critical desire had been published.[15] The subject of Sebald's critical reception and the pleasure so many (myself included) have taken in the aesthetics of his texts pose important if perhaps presently unanswerable questions, not least of which is how we address and explain (and that we feel we might need or want to) the quality, space, and work of desire that has come to circulate around Sebald's name and writings.[16] If an attempt to explain this minor discursive explosion (it remains, after all, something of a niche market) remains premature and problematic, this is less a function of the recentness of the phenomenon or of a lack of what is sometimes called critical distance. Is not the fantasy of critical distance one in which the object, or the text as finished work, must be sufficiently steeped in history, symbolically entombed for a posterity that would only reaffirm an already established stamp of legitimacy? Under such terms, criticism would appear fated to merely worship the object as sacred or fetishize its auratic surplus value. In either case, the presumption of proper distance is a way of sublimating, or taking distance from, the difficult question of how the critic's desire participates in aesthetic experience and critical judgment. The fantasy of critical distance and the problem of (not) possessing adequate measure for externalizing and reading critical desire do not present themselves here for the first time. In the terms Woolf uses to read her contemporary literary-critical scene, at stake is the question of reading the not-yet-sealed-off or conventionally sanctioned desires of criticism, particularly in a historical context that takes shape primarily in the contradiction between a sense of accelerated fragmentation and the consolidating forces of the market. In the space of this tension, Woolf places the affirmative accent of the modern in what it has yet to synthesize, an open or negatively presented space of the "new" that represents the only possibility for the aesthetic's historical self-reflection. "Every day we find ourselves doing, saying, or thinking things that would have been impossible to our fathers. And we feel the differences which have not been noted far more keenly than the resemblances which have been very perfectly expressed."[17]

And yet, we are no longer of Woolf's moment; the notion of the illegible, yet-to-be-formulated difference of the new, still necessary to placing hope in the future, is inimical to the tone and world of Sebald's prose. Far from being invested in the future, Sebald's novel seems to want nothing at all, other than the repose of death.

"Skirting"

The Rings of Saturn situates itself somewhere on the outskirts of world and genre, tracing in departure the literary-terrestrial terrains of the travel diary, recollections of the walking tour, memoir of a life beyond. The uncertain terrain of the narrator's movement blurs physical landscape with mental theater, wandering between space of encounter and layered dislocations of the writing event. A text of traversals, it moves across, splicing itineraries, forging gaps in language, time, memory, place.

Sebald's journey takes place in a world everywhere marked by traces of destruction, abandonment, ruin, and decay. The text begins with a framing account in which the narrator recalls setting off on a walking tour of "the county of Suffolk, in the hope of dispelling the emptiness that takes hold of me whenever I have completed a long stint of work" (3). Abandoned to the void that defines and undermines the posterity of the completed work (a familiar note from Woolf's diaries and Blanchot's essays), the writer, giving voice to an "emptiness," begins a story of walking tour as walking cure and yet immediately goes on to dispel the expectation that such "hopes" as were his are to find fulfillment, the reassuring comfort (and then again discomfort; as he has already acknowledged, completion is not always the pleasure one might have hoped for) of a desire brought toward its anticipated end.[18] Neither the walk nor the completed work of *this* work, the work of writing, are to sustain the hope of curative fulfillment, the goal of culminating repose. And just as the threat of an expanding "emptiness" is not so easily bracketed, neither will it be possible to locate or exteriorize the place of origin, the subject or past out of which (or, with equal uncertainty of mimetic accent, after which) the work of writing takes off.

Thus, a repetition of setting out, as the narrative, once more, and still near the outset, reaches back to recall another point of departure, the perforated scene of writing's emergence. Looking backward, speculating on the journey across Suffolk that is, for him, already in the past, he speaks as if from the other side of madness.

> At all events, in retrospect I became preoccupied not only with the unaccustomed sense of freedom but also with the paralyzing horror that had come over me at various times when confronted with the traces of destruction, reaching far back into the past, that were evident even in that remote place. Perhaps it was because of this that, a year to the day after I began my tour I was taken into hospital in Norwich in a state of almost total immobility. It was then that I began my thoughts to write these pages. (4)

Palliative detour notwithstanding, *The Rings of Saturn* is more than a fiction of the writing cure; whatever the account of the work's history of occasion, it is also a work of repetition, a return to "traces of destruction" and the alluring hallucination of the void. The text will return, again and again, to a temporality of circularity and repetition. The recollected image of an emptiness at outset, a kind of lack in departure, will return in scenes of suspended privation: splintered fragments of a world in vanishing, "all that remains" of a vastness of dispersal, destruction without end (30). A world "imperceptibly nearing the brink of dissolution and silent oblivion" (36), a world on the verge of an encroaching annihilation and the impossible, entropic nothingness of finitude.

From "peregrinate, v. 1. *intr.* To travel, journey; to go from place to place. Also *fig.* 2. *intr.* To reside abroad. *Obs. Rare.* 3. *trans.* To travel along, across, or around; to traverse."[19] The etymological trace, driving ahead to the "pilgrim," and *le pelerin*, is useful, as it takes us to the novel's opening epigraph, a citation in which a figure of the walking pilgrimage, *le pèlerinage à pied*, will introduce a scene of suffering and a call for forgiveness. As we will see in a moment, the epigraph, which is attributed to one of Joseph Conrad's letters, emerges as a way of looking at things, setting up a tension between those unfortunate ones who look without understanding (*qui regardent sans comprendre*) and those who, standing apart and looking from a slightly different angle, might see something else besides. Conrad will not say for certain whether the difference has anything to do with seeing from above or with attaining higher ground. At stake, not surprisingly given the trope of pilgrimage, are questions of the making of the path, the derivation and direction of the pilgrim's progress, the symbolization of the journey, and the writing of a writer-traveler's-narrator's desire.

Attributed to Joseph Conrad, from a "letter to Marguerite Poradowska, 23rd–25th March 1890," the epigraph makes a case for a demand, a demand for forgiveness. *"Il faut surtout pardonner à ces âmes malheureuses qui ont élu de faire le pèlerinage à pied, qui côtoient le rivage et regardent sans comprendre l'horreur de la lutte, la joie de vaincre ni le profound désespoir des vaincus."*[20] Shuttling from epigraph to the text and back again, it is quite difficult, and, as with any epigraph, not necessarily productive or even possible, to make one scan in terms of the other. The epigraph is a fragment that floats, a paratext hovering on the margins of the narrative journey that follows. Like those who "skirt the shore, *côtoient le rivage*," the epigraph clings to the text by a kind of skirting, maintaining proximity with remove, the adjacency of the edge. Alternatively part of and on the border of the shore (*le rivage*, cognate of border, skirt, margin), the epigraph outlines a path of mixed resistance, a reluctance in joining, an opening dehiscence.[21] From this scene of splitting, the pouring open of words as if from a wound, the text introduces a language of unforgivable suffering.

The epigraph introduces a strange notion of a pilgrimage manqué, a pilgrimage made in the breach, on the outskirts, with indirection, and on foot (the latter, despite the figurative implication of a privative relationship to a different scene, another path and alternative way to go, is fitting to the anachronism implied in "making a pilgrimage," a phrasing of the "journey" that is no longer current; as Sebald writes at one point, "I felt like a journeyman in a century gone by . . . every foot traveler incurs the suspicion of the locals, especially nowadays" [175]). The sense of a diverted movement that is nonetheless a movement forward, a movement alongside yet oblique to a path toward an end, is divided, and more than once. There is the sense of the pilgrimage as devotional journey to a sacred destination and then the sense of pilgrimage as an event of endless wandering, an itinerancy without any clear path toward outcome.

Sebald's journey takes place against a backdrop of destruction, vanishing, perishing, extinction, exhaustion, decay, and obsolescence. What remains of the world takes shape as ruin, detritus, and fragment, invoking the abyss of a final disappearance. It is as if our narrator were witness to a panoramic still life of history as it nears its end, where the terminus is less an effect of apocalyptic punctuation than of a cumulative, if not quite meaningful, process of winding down, lessening, exhaustion. For instance, in his account of his journey to Somerleyton Hall, the narrator recalls a deserted, diminished train station. A station that isn't a station. After descending from the train,

> The train ground into motion again and disappeared round a gradual bend, leaving a trail of black smoke behind it. There was no station at the stop, only an open shelter. I walked down the deserted platform, to my left the seemingly endless expanses of the marshes and to my right, beyond a low brick wall, the shrubs and trees of the park. There was not a soul about, of whom one might have asked the way. (31)

There is a sense of isolation and melancholy, a place characterized by what is missing, structures and people not there. As the passage continues, the narrator fills up the space with an image of its past.

> At one time, I thought, as I slung my rucksack over my shoulder and crossed the track, things would have been quite different here. Almost everything a residence such as Somerleyton required for its proper upkeep and all that was necessary in order to sustain a social position never altogether secure would have been brought in on the railway from other parts of the country and would have arrived at this station in the goods van of the olive-green-liveried steam train—furnishings, equipment and impedimenta of every description, the new piano, curtains and portieres, the Italian tiles and fittings for the bathrooms, the boiler and pipes for the hothouses, supplies from the market gardens, cases of hock and Bordeaux, lawn mowers and great boxes of whalebone corsets and crinolines from London. And now there was nothing any more, nobody, no stationmaster in gleaming peaked cap, no servants, no coachman, no house guests, no shooting parties, neither gentlemen in indestructible tweeds nor ladies in stylish traveling clothes. It takes just one awful second, I often think, and an entire epoch passes. (31)

The passage combines elegiac lyricism with an odd sense of a researched knowledge, the last caretaker of a ruined world.

The Horizontal and the Strange

> Strange things happen when you aimlessly wander through the world, when you go somewhere and then just want to see what happens next.
>
> W. G. Sebald, " 'But the Written Word Is Not a True Document' "

> What is certain, though, is that mental suffering is effectively without end. One may think one has reached the very limit, but there are always more torments to come. One plunges from one abyss into the next.
>
> W. G. Sebald, *The Emigrants*

Among the challenging effects of Sebald's prose is its masterful suspension of any one hierarchy or scene of significance. Even in its two dominant forms of interest—variations on reading the document, the record, remains of the past in traces; and the return of scenes of senseless destruction, mass death, and abandonment—a tension inheres between repetition and difference, commonality and lack of connection. In its staging of an openness to the encounter with whatever presents itself along the way (even and precisely when "whatever" appears as return to forms of disaster and decline), the text partakes of that line of novelistic realism whose primary conceit, rather than a coherence driven by "criteria of verisimilitude and appropriateness," is instead suggestive of a "loss of representative proportions and proprieties. . . . [E]verything is now on the same level, the great and the small, important events and insignificant episodes, human beings and things. Everything is equal, equally representable."[22]

In its scattering of images, events, and partial recollections, Sebald's text effects a form of bringing together, a conjoining of the various along the way. Strangely silent on its own procedures of attachment, selection, and collection, the text encourages, one might even say it compels, us to ask, How are we to read such acts of making way, of holding open the space of encounter, and toward what end its peregrinating movements? According to what logic, if any, does the work gather, collect, and emplace any one text or any thing (thought fragment, found object, delocalized and perhaps representative image) alongside any other? If, as is perhaps obvious, it is only the work of gathering that brings together, tenuously and without any obvious (curatorial?) strategy or rule, pieces of memory, part objects torn from uncertain worlds and often of unclear authorship, provenance, or origin, how do we read the form and desire of such a singular gathering? Picking up pieces of text, history, objects found, and stories from others, the narrator and narrative move along, as if for no purpose other than to have done so in whatever form, to have been there without prior purpose or plan. "There," the itinerary of a wandering, the writing of the desire to drift. The drift of a desire whose aim, in Kantian terms, finds itself somewhere between the purely formal (a direction or path akin to Kant's notion of teleology as purposiveness without purpose) and the pathological (an interest that would "belong" to the subject alone).

Splicing continuities with the horizontal, metonymic drift of association ("this" and then "this," where the connection between any two such moments, to the extent that such a connection comes to mind as question, is usually sutured with the sparse indeterminacy of a "perhaps"), the narrative presents only a bare, nearly vanishing lattice of contiguity. At the same time, the figure of a lattice—the form of the quincunx, for example—is both too strong and conceptually insufficient. It implies an order of geometry, the notion of a stable, preexisting, and patterned form that, even if imperceptibly, would hold the logic of the work together, giving rule to an otherwise minimalist presentation of the binding effects, to the order of parts made to connect as a whole. Rather more helpful, I think, to invoke a word Virginia Woolf uses so frequently in her writings on Sir Thomas Browne, whose interest in, among other things, the figure of the quincunx, is cited by Sebald's narrator. Browne's prose, Woolf writes, is interesting because it remains altogether *strange*.[23] The strange: a homely word for the unfamiliar, or, better, a resolutely vernacular and conceptually undistinguished word for reflecting on the emergence of the new and unassimilated at the margins of established forms and zones of comfort.[24]

The Rings of Saturn is certainly a strange text, in part because the quality of its estrangement—for instance, the singularity that differentiates it from any simple categorization within a genre—maintains an out-of-placeness not easily pinned down. Genre will not resolve the question of reading this work of recollection, the writer's collection of memories gathered over the course of a walking tour, a course taken down in notes that are sifted and reread and formalized later, as we are told in the text's frame of outsetting ("Now that I begin to assemble my notes," the narrator writes [5]). If we call it a scrapbook, we have done no more than emphasize a presentation that holds together through the bare, nonhierarchical texture of parataxis: the stitch as nonhierarchical addition, the syntactical link that refuses subordination through the raw spacing of the "and," a temporizing diachrony predicated on the minimal joints of "next" and "then." Parataxis itself implies something of a rhetorical law, the rule of leveling thought in style, or as Adorno, following Benjamin, defines its "striking" appearance in Hölderlin's late work, the "artificial disturbances that evade the logical hierarchy of a subordinating syntax."[25] In Sebald's prose, the artifice of the additive conjunction is hardly obvious. Abstracting from the understanding of parataxis as syntactical suspension of the logic of connection, one can say that the ordering of something like a path—both geographical itinerary and direction of thought—conspicuously raises and avoids the questions that are implied, in this case in suspension, by the notion of a "logical hierarchy" of order and meaning, including the hierarchy that would give privileged place to a logic of intention. In other words, the critical power of parataxis, which points to the disjointed forms of conjoining in the movement of Sebald's prose, returns us to the questions, How does one step, turn, or stop along the way relate to another? And what constitutes the "unit" of any "one"?

The figure of a scrapbook, in part because of its homely and feminine connotations, is a helpful turn, as it keeps us on the question of reading the work as collection—and moreover, a collection of material detritus, leftovers, and fragments, the accumulated quasi-archival stuff called scrap. To collect—to bring together, to stick alongside, to glue. What might it mean to figure Sebald's narrator as a collector, the text as collection? Of the collector, Benjamin notes, "Perhaps the most deeply hidden motive of the person who collects can be described this way: he takes up the struggle against dispersion."[26] Our narrator is moved by this struggle, but it is less clear that his motive is to work against it. What he takes up is often no more and no less than what happens to come to mind.

Thus, for instance, the story of one Major George Wyndham Le Strange is introduced by a familiar, one might even say a Sebaldian, moment of "perhaps," a loose and noncommittal speculative and rhetorical leap that cuts into even as it constitutes a bridge of connection. "Perhaps it was that darkening [of the sky] that called to my mind an article I had clipped from the *Eastern Daily Press* several months before, on the death of Major George Wyndham Le Strange, whose great stone manor house in Henstead stood beyond the lake. During the last War, the report read, Le Strange . . ." (59). I will come back to the figure—and the name—of Le Strange, who, as Sebald recalls reading and as a subsequently photographically documented newspaper clipping will attest, "served in the anti-tank regiment that liberated the camp at Bergen Belsen on the 14th of April 1945" (59, 63). First, however, let us return to the moment just before Le Strange's appearance. The scene draws on the visual topography of the pastoral and picturesque's rhetoric of the "painted" landscape. Sebald, having "reached Benacre Broad, a lake of brackish water beyond a bank of shingle halfway between Lowestoft and Southwold," reflects on what he saw.

> The lake is encircled by deciduous woodland that is now dying, owing to the steady erosion of the coastline by the sea. Doubtless it is only a matter of time before one stormy night the shingle bank is broken, and the appearance of the entire area changes. But that day, as I sat on the tranquil shore, it was possible to believe one was gazing into eternity. The veils of mist that drifted inland that morning had cleared, the vault of the sky was empty and blue, not the slightest breeze was stirring, the trees looked painted, and not a single bird flew across the velvet-brown water. It was as if the world were under a bell jar, until great cumulous clouds brewed up out of the west casting a grey shadow upon the earth. (59)

And with this recollection of revelation in quietude, an unveiling of the transient as the eternal, Sebald's thoughts take a turn. A cloud, something like a swerve, appears out of the blue; reading backwards, it becomes the textual occasion for the turn to Le Strange, a darkening connection, "perhaps."

Yet, before drawing a distinction between one scene and the other, let us recall that it is the question of such a distinction that we are pursuing. (In English the typography of a paragraph break helps create the unit of difference, whereas in the German there is no such break.)[27] Reading the passage above and the multiply refracted story of Le Strange together does not mean stabilizing their relationship through a third term of commensuration: Neither nature nor the natural-historical link of a complicit "darkening" will provide a meaningful logic for the relationship. The question is how they might cohere and differ, and how the text, by presenting them in a flowing diachrony of thought, gives us to think them as existents in the same world, the world as if "under a bell jar." Like the world bound yet dissociated in the pages of a torn-up scrapbook, *The Rings of Saturn* presents fragments torn from more than one elsewhere, juxtaposed, brought together, and made visible by the figure of the collector—a participant-observer walking through the land of the dead.

As "collector of oddities" (36) in his own right, Sebald's narrator, ever-receding yet always present, the voice through whom all others speak, yet a voice minimally articulated in its justifications, inclinations, and choices, is something of an oddity himself. The narrator—and this is perhaps Sebald's singular genius as well as a condition of his wide-ranging critical reception—manages to be more than usually attached to the ground (enough to set out on foot in a world where walking has become an anachronism), while at the same time disappearing behind the stories and objects he presents. Less a distinct subject or a character than an occasion for the encounter with what presents itself as if by chance, the narrator appears, to cite one of many such phrases, as if "imperceptibly nearing the brink of dissolution and silent oblivion" (36). The narrator—with a frustratingly inapposite balance of patience and indifference—is an imperceptible flourish, something like the Neutral, as Barthes has used the term.[28]

Atrocity Supplements (Reprise)

When *The Rings of Saturn* reproduces a photograph taken by the British photographer George Rodger in April 1945, it neither gives nor denies attribution to the name of the photograph's author-producer. Presented alongside the story of Major George Wyndham Le Strange, the photograph draws at least some of its force from a tension that inheres in Sebald's prose: the uncertainty surrounding the (citational, archival, fictional) status of the image as document.

The image-objects reproduced in Sebald's *The Rings of Saturn* often float in an indeterminate suspense of citation: Without the anchoring procedures of the caption, and in some cases untethered to conventional forms of reference matter (the contextualizing supplement of attribution, the performative contradiction of reference to source; the fiction of an unbroken line from image to origin, the image as if attached to its *provenance*), the images dislodge iterability from the grounding demands of authenticity, verifiability, and authorized use. Without the acutely self-recursive irony of any distinctly postmodern "turn," the text blurs the line between archive and fiction, dislocating the place of the image and its relation to the categories of the historical and the invented.[29] Sebald's style of citation, borrowing, and reuse (both of images and of text), his presentation of material taken from others, conspicuously resists explicit and conventional procedures, refusing to mark, frame, leverage, claim, and justify the act of citation with standard provisions of additional documentation. Such suspension of the rules is part of the play.

Although all the images that appear in Sebald's prose are presented without caption, they are not all equally detached from signifying frames of reference. Thus, for instance, in Sebald's iterative appropriation of the language of Conrad's *Heart of Darkness*, the name of the author is as much given as presumed (117–20). Similarly, in the discussion of Rembrandt's *The Anatomy Lesson*, woven into a speculation on the possibility of Thomas Browne's having present at the scene of the spectacle, there "among the onlookers in the anatomy theatre in Amsterdam" (17), when the text twice reproduces the image of Rembrandt's painting, the name of the artist is hardly at issue. (Rather, the narrative is invested in the identification and direction of the artist's gaze. An interesting tension inheres within the passage: between blindness and insight, a dissimulated void and the revealed meaning of the signifier. Its overall effect is to suggest that the narrator, like Rembrandt, is invested in leaving traces of otherwise unrecognized violence—perhaps to the body of the corpse—and exposing misprisions of victimization in his text.)[30]

On the page, uncaptioned and without any explicitly tethered textual exposition, Rodger's photograph as it appears in Sebald's text is minimally anchored in the narrative through the story of Major George Wyndham

Le Strange. As recounted first by the narrator and later by the reproduction of a press clipping in the text (the clipping becomes archive-docu-
ment-object-image-text all at once), the story of Le Strange is, indeed,
strange. The narrator's account slips seamlessly from a moment of recall
and reading, a recollection of a recollection ("Perhaps it was that darkening that called to my mind an article I had clipped from the *Eastern Daily
Press* several months before, on the death of Major George Wyndham Le
Strange, whose great stone manor house in Henstead stood beyond the
lake"), into a presentation of the account as if verbatim from the article as
well as from knowledge gathered from other sources. The passage continues, "During the last War, the report read, Le Strange served in the anti-
tank regiment that liberated the camp at Bergen Belsen on the 14th of
April 1945, [photograph, covering a full two facing pages] but immediately
after VE-Day returned home from Germany to manage his great uncle's
estates in Suffolk, a task he had fulfilled in exemplary manner, at least until
the mid-Fifties, as I knew from other sources" (61–62). In the English
edition, the photograph appears in the midst of these sentences, as indi-
cated in brackets.

The image covers two facing pages of the text. Its upper two-thirds are
dominated by large trees whose branches extend beyond the frame. As the
eye follows the vertical trunks of the trees downward, below the branch
line, the trees begin to occupy and render visible another world. On the
ground are heaps of matter, some of it draped, blanketed, yet not fully
covered. Toward the left of the image, one shape lends a shadow of legibil-
ity to the rest. It looks something like a human skeleton. Corpses. Heaps
of dead bodies. Unburied remains.

Much has been written on the appearance of this image in the text,
as well as on its placement within, or rather adjacent to, the narrative's
presentation of the stories related to the life and death of Major Le
Strange. I will discuss some of that criticism in greater detail in a moment,
but first I want to note that the text's unforged connection to George
Rodger has been upheld, repeated, even extended, and more dubiously
mystified in the criticism on the novel. For one critic, it is manifestly impossible that the photograph exists at all, and if it does, it can only be "as
a simulation similar to the photographic collections of Christian Boltanski," an absurd yet productively problematic argument whose implications
I will try to address below.[31]

I consider the link to Rodger as suspended by the text. The connection
is not explicitly denied, nor is any prior awareness of it presupposed. I

certainly do not want to suggest that we posit the image's history of production and reproduction (its other history, as it were), over against its
appearance in *The Rings of Saturn*, giving the archival to hold sway in a
revealed priority. On the contrary, it is only because of Sebald's text that
I found my way to Rodger's image, and then to its story. And this story is
not entirely clear to me, even now. Reading the image on its face (and of
course it is precisely the image of the human rendered faceless, bringing
me to wonder: Can there be such a thing as postmortem abjection?) or in
the context of other information, such as the story George Rodger tells of
the experience of shooting this image, or the fact that the bodies in the
photograph would end up, at some point between April 20, 1945, and
April 28, the day the "backlog of corpses was finally cleared," in a mass
grave, I am reminded of a phrase Benjamin uses in "The Storyteller."
Writing of the unprecedented, and unassimilated, scale-effects of mechanized warfare, Benjamin, precisely without sentimentality and indeed with
some ambivalence, leaves us with an image of material remains, perhaps
newly deformed and diminished in presence: the "tiny, fragile human
body." Only, of course, these bodies are not those of soldiers.[32]

The story of the image taken by George Rodger in April 1945 is interesting not because it gives us more knowledge about Bergen-Belsen in the
days after its liberation (or about the conditions that prevailed before-
hand), for such information has been gathered and retold elsewhere. Borrowing a phrase that *The Rings of Saturn* borrows from Sir Thomas
Browne, I might say that the photograph tells a story of the "iniquity
of oblivion," a mixed, ambivalent, and negatively phrased gloss on the
nonrelation between justice and survival, ethical meaning and symbolic
posterity, future dissemination of the name. "Survival" in this sense can
refer both to living-on in life, to survival before death, and to the symbolic
afterlife of memory, reputation, fame. The "iniquity of oblivion," then is
not only the arbitrariness of the success of being remembered rather than
forgotten but also the injustice of death's (non)arrival, the lack of fairness
in not being able to die, not yet and not now, of having to continue on.
As Sebald invokes Browne, both of these senses of the phrase are suggested: "To set one's name to a work gives no one a title to be remembered, for who knows how many of the best of men have gone without a
trace? The iniquity of oblivion blindly scatters her poppy seed and when
wretchedness falls upon us one summer's day like snow, all we wish for is
to be forgotten" (24).[33]

One might object, does not the gross generality of such a proxima-
tion—setting one citation from the text (the photograph) alongside another (the interpolation of Browne's text), especially when the two are

distant in narrative placement and time—does not such a reading through juxtaposition reduce the gravity of the Holocaust, as metonymically invoked through the photograph and its association with Bergen-Belsen, to Browne's eclectic yet ultimately Christian theodicy, which rationalizes "iniquity" and "oblivion" in deference to the deferred judgment of the divine? Such is one of the possible leveling effects of Sebald's prose, particularly if one follows the narrator in his performance of a naive exhaustion: Having suspended any sustained desire to interpret the world, the narrator leaves the reader with only the barest common thread linking his narrative fragments, a residual thematics of melancholy, loss, and injustice as the "way of the world."

And yet, the photograph, irreducible to the rest, produces an effect—and questions—of its own. Indeed the image, all the more so with Rodger's history (semi)attached to it, points to what some have called the turning point in the history of images: the moment when photography came to stand in for truth in the failure of words.[34] If that history was indeed a turning point, it returns here in a hyperbolic performativity of the principle that shows its effacement (Figure 2).

As for the reasons the unmarked (dis)connection has not been noticed in the scholarship, one might speculate that it has simply not been considered of sufficient interest to mention, but, as we will see, this does not appear to be the case. Perhaps the photographer's name, career, and work are simply not widely known.[35] Perhaps it is an issue of the medium itself; as has often been suggested, photography, both in its reproducibility and in its indexicality (or what might be considered its documentary or referential function, such that it bears an order of "the Intractable," or what Barthes famously describes as the photograph's "scandalous effect," unique among other "systems of representation," to attest undeniably that, at some point in the past, "*That-has-been*"),[36] maintains less of a relationship with its author-producer than with what is on the surface, with what the photograph records, the momentary past it reproduces as frozen image. Thus, the question of how the photograph came into being might give way before the sheer fact of *what* the image bears witness to and *that* it has done so, as if mechanically and without consideration for any extra documentary space or demand, for instance, the demand that might be placed on, and raised by, the image, such as a viewer's, reader's, or editor's desire for further documentation, or for any other form of textual matter or explanatory elaboration.[37] Perhaps, especially in the context of such a signifier (Bergen-Belsen) and such an event (if it can be thought of this way, as being of a kind), issues related to the history of the image—

Figure 2. George Rodger, "Bodies at Bergen-Belsen." (Time & Life Pictures/Getty Images.)

including the name of its photographer, the conditions under which the photographer was present at the scene, the dates and names of publications in which the image has appeared in the past, and the current status of its copyright—are distinct and separable from the more immediate visual totality (however partial we know it to be) of what the image insists on, of what it gives us to see. Finally—and this is the only one of the conjectural explanations I find plausible—one might speculate, in the case of the image under discussion, that the nature of the image itself, its uncanny mixture of beauty (formal symmetry, arboreal transcendence, nature's grandeur and reposefulness) *and* unthinkable horror (with a pause on mention of "sublimity," I will note, for the moment, the horrific "discovery" in the detail, signs not only of life's petrification but of privation so extreme that description does indeed seem pointless, one might say hopelessly, grotesquely inadequate: signs of starvation, of exposure, of mortification in every sense of the word; perhaps above all the corpses, dumped and splayed out like so much trash, countless and impossible to individuate, shock and horrify us in our gaze, for thus they are exposed to the elements and the world, the remains of the *unburied* dead), perhaps this unsettling image, in what must be recognized as not only its documentary but also its mixed aesthetic effects, is more than unbearable, imposing on us more than we want to recognize or less (ethical certainty?) than we want to allow, and for these and other reasons it would be rather easier to hope that no such photograph was ever taken, that no such image could possibly exist.

As Daub notes, Sebald sometimes "unhinges his photographs from their real object. This calls into question whether the photographs, whether supposedly archival or family snapshots, have not been similarly transplanted—whether a picture of a liberated Bergen Belsen is not perhaps one of Birkenau instead. What Sebald's technique thus radically brackets is the indexicality of the mode of production itself."[38] One of the effects of the indexical, or pointing, function of the photographic image is to signify something like *"This* was," where both the "this" and the "was" point not only to the frozen haecceity of the contents of the image but also to the photographic apparatus and history that brings forth the image as suspended afterlife of the event, a framed bit of the past haunted by the mortal time it has symbolically displaced but can never forestall or reverse. The indexical function says, *"This* was (taken, seen, recorded by a photographic apparatus)." In the case of the image under discussion, to say that the indexical function has collapsed is to imply that the image points to a "thisness" that may never have been at all. Not only might the photograph not be an image of Belsen, it might never have been taken. No such photograph exists.

"There are literally hundreds of pictures taken on or around the day Allied forces liberated Bergen Belsen. . . . None of them, however, have the particular dynamic of the image Sebald chooses."[39] Such a claim to comprehensive knowledge of the totality of the archives is remarkable, even by standards of scholarly research. The critic's desire to insist on the archival inexistence of the image attests to the photograph's noniconic status, a relative unrecognizability that reminds us of the indelible predominance of those very few, so often repeated, images that have come to "stand (in) for" the Holocaust, the vastness of its atrocities notwithstanding (and, for some, despite the critical understanding that no such representative totality is available): One thinks, for instance, of Margaret

Bourke-White's famous image of male survivors standing behind barbed wire at Buchenwald or the ominous image of a depopulated Birkenau, with its train tracks pointing the viewer's eye toward the entrance gate, taken by Stanislaw Mucha.[40]

That both the Bourke-White and the Mucha images and the image taken by Rodger and reproduced by Sebald were taken at the liberation of the camps points to the historical displacement of the problem of representing the otherwise unrepresented, and for some, the unrepresentable, events and brutality of the camps. This problem, which has been extensively discussed by theorists of the Holocaust and its aftermath, still "probes," to invoke Saul Friedlander's phrase, the significance, and the limited returns of, acknowledging the "limits of representation." While the debates surrounding these issues are extremely nuanced and complicated, they can be loosely schematized as follows: There is the question of reading the historical asymmetry of the archive, or the effects of the differential possibilities for photographic documentation and witnessing. In part, such differences can be read in terms of the division, temporal and dialectical, effected through the opening that liberation produced. The images of the camps, as they became available for dissemination and iconization are, in a sense, necessarily afterimages, limited to "what remained" when and after the Allies entered camps. That they should represent the entirety of the history of all that came before them is part of their burden and their limitation. That they recast, retrospectively and to strong purpose for the Allies going forward (if only for a time and if differently in each country) the figure of the German as an enemy so horrific that the war became, after all, justified, has been well demonstrated.[41]

Along with the question of how liberation photographs have been privileged in the historical symbolization of the Holocaust, and of how they have, to an extent, been made to do the symbolic work of "standing (in) for" a history that both precedes and remains evident in them, a history that they represent but that they also begin to frame as past, there is the related problematic of reading and representing all that remains—without remains, vanished life—as well as the traces and remnants and incomplete narratives that can never restore or make fully present the whole story, however we may imagine it. The fact that there are, in Didi-Huberman's phrasing, "images after all" of the crematoria at Auschwitz has renewed the debate over how to read and represent the history of an otherwise annihilated memory of annihilation.[42]

Writing of the iconic status of certain images from the Holocaust archives, in other words of the dominance of a very narrow and repetitive repertoire of a few photographs shown as representative images, Marianne Hirsch has observed,

> The repeated Holocaust photographs connect past and present through the "having-been-there" of the photographic image. They are messengers from a horrific time that is not distant enough. In repeatedly exposing themselves to the same pictures, postmemorial viewers can produce in themselves the effects of traumatic repetition that plague the victims of trauma. Even as the images repeat the trauma of looking, they disable, in themselves, any restorative attempts.[43]

One wonders how to read Hirsch's use of the verb "can" ("postmemorial viewers *can* produce in themselves the effects of traumatic repetition"), and what to make of the "ability" it implies. As a description of the possible, the passage suggests a neutral, nonaffirmative and nonpathologizing, take on the repetition at work in such identificatory production of more trauma. Yet the resistance to the restorative, so important to the maintenance of trauma's return to the scene of a wound, suggests a kind of critical embrace of this deferral. As the passage continues, we can read precisely this tension between an embrace of traumatic repetition (again, perhaps descriptively, simply to suggest that as psychic and cultural phenomenon, such repetition, in any case, already takes place) and a critical reframing of a compulsive fascination with the suffering of the victim and the representation of death.

> It is only when they [the images] are redeployed, in new texts and new contexts, that they *regain* a capacity to enable a postmemorial working through. The aesthetic strategies of postmemory are specifically about such an attempted, and yet an always postponed, repositioning and reintegration.[44]

If these are indeed the stakes, Sebald suggests that postmemory offers us no guarantee that the image will not become a fetish. More interestingly, there is no guarantee that looking at a photograph of corpses will tell us more than we want to recognize.

"There is no photograph that does not turn its 'subject' to ruins."[45] In this case, the "subject" is between death and burial, a photograph of the remains, reproduced to float in iterative disorientation in a narrative from another place and time. There is no way to read this gesture other than as an aesthetics of provocation, which would mean investing it (one might say in a paranoid fashion) with a desire to test, prod, and cross a limit. It is a wildly demonstrative desacralization, a refusal to adhere to any ban on aestheticizing images of the dead. (Sebald might have chosen any number of other images by Rodger in which more information and context are available. This image is exceptional for its lack of any enframed viewer, as so many of the photographs are images of others taking photographs, of other people looking on in horror, of the Germans from neighboring towns being forced to come to see the evidence. Such procedures of enframing provide the viewer with the cover of another, already "outside" viewer to mediate the violence and desire of the gaze. Other images provide more narrative information: for instance, images of German guards brutally carrying the corpses of their former inmates, throwing them into mass graves. The contradiction of such images: Although the British want to enjoy their victory and want to demonstrate their military and moral triumph over the smug and mighty Germans, the images of German officers being made to do their bidding, however humiliated the Germans may be, are still images of German officers heaving thousands of corpses into a pit. Perhaps Sebald simply found such images too obvious in their potential provocatory function.)

Sebald's aesthetics mixes the sublime with the naive. For Moses Mendelssohn, the latter is appropriate to what he considers the objective sublime, or those ideas, experiences, and objects that are, in themselves, "so perfect, so sublime that they cannot be reached by any finite thought, cannot be adequately intimated by means of any sign, and cannot be represented as they are by any images. Among such things are God, the world, eternity, and so on."[46] For such things, Mendelssohn argues, the naive is the only affecting means of presenting the already full condition of sublimity. "Thus, in representing something sublime of this type, the artist must devote himself to a naive, unaffected expression which allows the reader or spectator to think more than is said to him."[47] The desire for "more" incited by Sebald's text is precisely an effect of the tension between the symbolic weight of the "thing" (and here we are at odds with Mendelssohn's strictly prerepresentational idiom for the "thing") and the withholding performed in the text in its refusal to "spin" or "anchor" or expressly supplement the image. The late sublime as it appears in Sebald's text is an effect of this tension.[48] Rather than effecting the reader's private act of completion, Sebald's naive sublime only calls on and produces more incompletion. This is its failure, its provocation, and its achievement.

Toward a Conclusion:
The In-Exhaustible Catastrophe

The air is full of sighs and cries. These are never lost: if you listen
carefully, with a sympathetic ear, you can hear them echoing forever
within the second sphere. The night is best: sometimes when you
have difficulty in falling asleep it is because your ears have been
reached by the cries of the dead which, like their writings, are open
to many interpretations.

J. M. COETZEE, *Waiting for the Barbarians*

The wrong implied in the last judgment: After what I have just said,
there is nothing else to say.—But you are saying it! What are you
adding to what has previously been said by declaring that there is
nothing more to add? You are adding either that the preceding phrase
was the last phrase, or else that the phrases to come after your "last"
phrase will be tautologies of prior phrases. The first explanation is
non-sense (the after-the-last); the second requires demonstrating that
there is no new phrase to come.

JEAN-FRANÇOIS LYOTARD, *The Differend*

We live in an age of exhaustion. That the lament of being exhausted has
itself become excruciatingly tired and tiring is all to the point. What remains to be said about the rhetoric and politics of exhaustion, particularly
after so many have declaimed the exhaustion of language, the end of art,
the beginning of the end of one history or another? Ours is an epoch of
proliferating epochalizations, an era suspended in multiplicities of belatedness and the indeterminacy of the post- as prefix: posthistorical, postrepre-
sentation, postmodern, poststructuralist, postmillennial, postapocalyptic,
postsecular, postcolonial, postfeminist, postwar, postevolutionary, post-
marxist, postpolitical, posthumanist, postironic, posttraumatic, postindus-
trial, postnational, postideological, postnature, postglobal, posthuman.
Such a list is neither exhaustive nor inclusive as a set; there is no metaform
for reading the prefix of the "post-." At the same time, the heterogeneity
of the aggregate does not exactly induce the kind of head-spinning vertigo,

bewilderment, or mental short-circuiting that has sometimes been associated, as in Lyotard's spin on the Kantian sublime, with language proliferating in resistance to norms of comprehensibility. Unlike the disquieting arrest that makes the sublime and its failure to cohere so compelling, the effect of drawing out the "post" in its multiple usages pushes us, if it moves us at all, only in circles around the thought of the symbolic in breakdown.

The endless effluvium of the "post": the intolerable void of the remainder; the inexhaustible, listless melancholy of the belated; the wearisome banality of the same. The negative edge-work that would articulate the post-as-rupture, and in which the diachrony of time would imply neither continuity with nor modular extension of a past imperative—such has been the burden of the post as it has forwarded, or stalled, a thinking of the event, the new, and the differences of futurity in the last decades of the last century. One way of approaching this burden, which has preoccupied critical thought as it has staked out various domains of the "after" and the "post" and the "beyond," is to consider the intense pressure brought to bear on criticism by the weight of its own epochalizing claims.[1]

The rhetoric of the break draws a line or crosses a step after which, in retrospect, it becomes possible to speak of the emergence of a difference inaugurated by the break itself; according to such a narrative, the irruptive event of the break could not have been predicted or thought prior to its emergence. The "post-" re-creates the past in its own terms, terms which find their relationality to the past only after they themselves have become part of the past. In this sense, the post does not indicate the exhaustion, completion, or teleological fulfillment of a prior epoch, logic, or set of terms. Rather it introduces a periodizing subsequency or afterward that itself, newly and as if out of the blue, posits and frames the past as whole, finite, over and done with, as if it were all washed out.

It is possible that one of the driving forces at work in the proliferation of fictions of the end of the world is the exhaustion with the interminability of exhaustion. If to be exhausted does not mean to have exhausted the all of time or the totality of the possible or to have found a way out of suffering existence, then it follows that the "more" that awaits—more time, more suffering, more work, more waiting, more desire, more exhaustion—imposes itself as both too much ("too much, too much," said the laboring body and exhausted figure of Mrs. McNab) and too little (a lack of a more meaningful alternative, a more effective way of living and dying, of a resolution to the "iniquity of oblivion," as Woolf and Sebald, borrowing from Thomas Browne, have put it).

By calling attention to exhaustion, and drawing out the place of catastrophe under an extended culture of lateness, I do not mean merely to reassert old oppositions between vigor and lassitude, morality and decadence, upstanding and degenerate life. Rather, exhaustion, as modality and temporality of endurance precisely at the limits of the endurable, when one can endure no more, as Deleuze has argued, imposes a critique of such oppositions.[2] To be exhausted is to experience the finitude of resources and, at the same time, in that experience, not to succumb to finishing, or to transcend the limit, but rather to exist between the longing for ending and the nonarrival of the end. Exhaustion in the form of completion, as in an exhaustive account or the making-present of a void—such forms of positivity and achievement are, like the idea of a well-lived death, variations on the enduring desire to exhaust the negativity of exhaustion.

It may be the case that literary scholarship has had enough of defining and redefining the boundaries, both historical and formal, of the modern; similarly, debates about the meaning of modernism, whether theorized as period or aesthetic ideology, may have reached a point of limited returns, an exhaustion of interest at least partially set in motion by modernism's own ambivalent investment in overcoming the problem of exhaustion. "We must reconcile ourselves to a season of failures and fragments. We must reflect that where so much strength is spent on finding a way of telling the truth, the truth itself is bound to reach us in rather an exhausted and chaotic condition."[3] Woolf's imperative for reconciliation stems not from a notion that everything has already been said (an idealist vision of totality, an exhaustive completion of the possible, a discourse of the all so often associated with modernist aesthetics). Rather, Woolf suggests, it is the thought of having already given voice to everything that modernism sets to work and calls into question. "What all intellectual disciplines and institutions presuppose is that not everything has been said, written down or recorded, that words already heard or pronounced are not the last words," Lyotard writes.[4] At stake within the modernist demand for the "new," however unrealized and perhaps essentially unrealizable this signatory desire may remain, a rhetoric of an in-exhausted aesthetics continues to assert itself through notions of inherited but obsolete forms and conventions modernism would seek to update, surpass, displace.

As so many critics of modernism have pointed out, the very oppositional logic that pits the new over against the old, indeed that writes the old *as* such, falls prey to its own structure of critique: On what basis, other than the sheer arbitrariness of a chronology in which the writers of the present succeed those of the past, does the modern differentiate and give priority to its own aesthetic practice and ideology? What, if anything, distinguishes the "now" of the present from that of the past, and for that matter from the "now" of the future? How is the modernist claim to reinvent, perhaps exhaustively, an old and exhausted aesthetic, not merely a prelude to another demand for yet a new form, a subsequent validation of the next over the last, in other words an ongoing series of repetitive, successive presentisms, each of which would reinscribe—but with what difference? And on what authority?—a narrative of epochal rupture and aesthetic revolution, claiming to have overturned the past even as it repeats its rhetoric? Adorno, wary of the demand that modernism settle the score of its differences, offers a critique of the mechanical critique of the fetish-character of the new.

> If a possibility for innovation is exhausted, if innovation is mechanically pursued in a direction that has already been tried, the direction of innovation must be changed and sought in another dimension. The abstractly new can stagnate and fall back into the ever-same. Fetishization expresses the paradox of all art that is no longer self-evident to itself.[5]

We can understand modernism's relation to the problem of exhaustion as twofold. In an affirmative sense, there is the desire to have done with the limit, in a sense to have exhausted—overcome and outlasted—previous definitions and enclosures of the possible. Affirming the possibility of extending literature beyond—beyond prior expectations, conventions, and formal ideals—literature would seek not merely to extend but to displace the limit (as Woolf notes, without limit, there would be no "catastrophe," no ending "in the accepted style").[6] At the same time, such an affirmative exhaustion requires that literature remain critical of any idealization of the new as the last, as the final realization—the exhaustion—of the possible. Even as it sets out to go beyond conservative claims by which the culture of the past becomes the exhaustive measure of cultural achievement tout court, modernism runs the risk of exhausting itself, in other words of claiming for itself just that position of completion it seeks to displace.

Deleuze, in a reading of Beckett, brings forward this twofold, incommensurate sense of exhaustion: In the first sense, exhaustion is the completion of a set, the reaching of a limit, the saturation of the possible, as in an exhaustive account, the reaching of the end of a finite series or resource, the attainment of a totality without exclusion or remainder. To exhaust as in reaching a point where there is "no more"—no more to say, know, consume, expend—no more space or words in which to realize new, alternative iterations of the possible. Exhaustion as finality. "The tired person has merely exhausted the realization, whereas the exhausted person exhausts the whole of the possible. The tired person can no longer realize, but the exhausted person can no longer possibilize."[7] The distinction between being tired and being exhausted—"Being exhausted is much more than being tired"—is only a preliminary elaboration of the significance of exhaustion in its twofold relationship to finitude, or, as Deleuze has it, exhaustion as both "the exhaustive *and* the exhausted."[8] As Deleuze reads exhaustion in Beckett, what interests him is the impossibility of realizing both of these together; the more exhaustive the account, the more exhausted the subject, and, concomitantly, the more impossible to get round the bend so as to finish finishing, so as to exhaust the question of what exhaustion would, in the last analysis, look like after the fact.

Thus, it is the problem of the inexhaustibility of exhaustion that constitutes the second, and for Deleuze the more interesting and more Beckettian, sense of thinking exhaustion. Deleuze calls this the problem of the "inclusive disjunction within a combinatorial," or the way in which the quest for exhaustive inclusiveness necessarily reaches a certain aporia, that impasse whereby any notion of realizing the last and final combination (here Deleuze is speaking primarily of a kind of ontolinguistic terminality, or "the ambition of the combinatorial [which] is to exhaust the possible with words") implies a falling-off of language, a becoming-silent, a failing to say more, while at the same time raising the question of how—through what next, what other combination of words, voices, utterances—to speak, declare, or otherwise bear witness to this event of the final combination? "What will be the last word, and how can it be recognized? . . . The aporia lies in the inexhaustible series of all these exhausted beings."[9]

The culture of lateness endures without surviving, continues without exhausting remainders new and old. If belatedness is an old plaint of modernity, a sense that so much time has passed, a feeling that all is behind us, we remain, perhaps, much the worse for the seeming inevitability of the repetitions on such a fictive disinheritance from history. When I think, for instance, of Alain Finkielkraut's articulation of a postwar affect of having missed the essential experience, the "experience of the horror," and the attendant "flaunting of a void," the void of the Holocaust as catastrophe *and*, moreover, as a catastrophe manqué, despite the specificity of the affect and its belated desire, I cannot help but recall echoes of the repetition, Marx's *Eighteenth Brumaire*.[10] So intransigent are the returns of the dead that we may, not for the first time, long to escape them. If belatedness signals a "parasitic" attachment to the past in its antipurposive and inertial weight—the weight of a past that is not yet over, the past that haunts us as the scene of so much unredeemed suffering, the past *as* the missed opportunity to make good on suffering—it also presents the desire for catastrophe all over again, this time a new and more exhaustive catastrophe, the revolution of an apocalypse that would not fail to disappoint.

NOTES

INTRODUCTION

1. Jean-Pierre Dupuy, *Pour un catastrophisme éclairé: Quand l'impossible est certain* (Paris: Éditions du Seuil, 2002), 17. Translation mine.

2. Karl Marx, *Grundrisse*, trans. Martin Nicolaus (London: Penguin, 1973), 524, 539.

3. Several critics have outlined a literary-historical shift in which, at some point between Thomas More's *Utopia* (1516) and the late nineteenth century, future-oriented writing took over the utopian tradition's generic function of imagining an other world. Or, as the argument goes, the locus of imagined otherness shifted from spatial to temporal projections. See, for instance, Ernst Bloch, "Something's Missing: A Discussion between Ernst Bloch and Theodor W. Adorno on the Contradictions of Utopian Longing," in *The Utopian Function of Art and Literature: Selected Essays*, trans. Jack Zipes and Frank Mechlenburg (Cambridge, Mass.: MIT Press, 1993), 3. Some critics construe the literary shift as explicitly coincident with a narrative of global, or European imperial, history, arguing that the exhaustion of "discoverable" space brought an end to the utopian tradition's spatialization of perfected alterity. Françoise Choay, in a study of the utopian tradition in architecture, coins the notion of "elsewhen" societies, arguing, "When the planet had been almost entirely explored, time was substituted for space as the 'no place' of utopia" (*The Rule and the Model: On the Theory of Architecture and Urbanism*, trans. Denise Bratton [Cambridge, Mass.: MIT Press, 1996], 408). See also H. G. Wells, "Utopias," *Science Fiction Studies* 27, no. 9 (1982): 120.

I. CATASTROPHE CULTURE, ATROCITY SUPPLEMENTS

1. *The Illustrated London News*, April 28, 1945, "Supplement," i. The paper features images of Nordhausen, Belsen, Buchenwald, and Langenstein as they were approached, liberated, taken over (although "liberated" has, of course, become the verb of record, there is room for expansion) by the British and American forces. For an extensive discussion of the uses of photography in constructing the narrative of the war, see Barbie Zelizer, *Remembering to Forget: Holocaust Memory through the Camera's Eye* (Chicago: University of Chicago Press, 1998).

2. Susan Sontag, *On Photography* (New York: Picador, 1977), 19–20.

3. Ibid. Sontag vaguely allows that such general anesthesia might have certain exceptions. "The ethical content of photographs is fragile. With the possible exception of photographs of those horrors, like the Nazi camps, that have gained the status of ethical reference points, most photographs do not keep their emotional charge" (21). Other critics, however, make the opposite claim, arguing that the repetition of certain, by now iconic, Holocaust images, rather than anchoring their singularly ethical status, functions to blunt the imagination and to provide an unacknowledged alibi for forgetting. See, for instance, Sybil Milton, "Images of the Holocaust," *Holocaust and Genocide Studies* 1, no. 1 (1986): 27–61. The rhetoric and problem of anesthetization raises larger questions about the impasses of exposure and memory, archivization and forgetting. The critical discourse on Holocaust memory is enormous, and my citations are selective. See Geoffrey Hartman's discussion of the paradoxes of "information sickness" in *The Longest Shadow: In the Aftermath of the Holocaust* (New York: Palgrave, 1996), 93–112. In a discussion directed specifically to the "psychic anesthesia" in the German postwar aesthetics of the banal, Benjamin Buchloh would seem to agree with Sontag that the images of the camps maintain an exceptional power, as demonstrated in Richter's *Atlas* project, where, Buchloh argues, they function as "a sudden revelation, namely that there is still one link that binds an image to its referent within the apparently empty barrage of photographic imagery and the universal production of exchange-value" ("Gerhard Richter's *Atlas*, The Anomic Archive," *October* 88 [Spring 1999]: 143–44).

4. In the atrocity supplement, the inscription of a logic of supplementarity takes place on several levels, of which the first to suggest itself is, perhaps, that of the photograph as supplement to the functional order and reliability of the printed word in narrative reportage. As supplement, in the critical and additive movement elaborated by Jacques Derrida (*Of Grammatology*, trans. Gayatri Chakravorty Spivak [Baltimore: Johns Hopkins University Press, 1988], esp. 144–64), the atrocity supplement calls attention to the photographic image as newly, singularly, and irreplaceably necessary to the newspaper's ability to deliver the story, to reveal the truth in its full and shocking horror. I return to this claim in the chapters that follow. For the moment, I simply note that *The Illustrated London News* is hardly alone in its investment, at precisely this moment (April and May 1945, in the moment and aftermath of the British and American "discovery" of the camps), in the discursive power and evidentiary weight of the photographic image. That the urgency and burning desire of this investment relies heavily on the framing typographics and anchoring techniques of the caption and headline (and occasionally name of source, whether individual photographer or representing agency), should give pause to any

notion that the photograph replaces or leaves the letter behind. Similarly, the unique force of the photographic image as substitutive witness comes forth and claims its irreplaceable place elsewhere, particularly in the oft-cited comments of the photographers. The statement of one of the British military photographers brings forth the paradoxical reversals of supplementarity at work in the visual imperative: "No words can describe the horror of this place. . . . I have read about camps like this, but never realised what it was really like. It must be seen to be believed" (Sgt. Midgley, letter in archives of Imperial War Museum, London, as cited in *The Face of the Enemy*, ed. Martin Caiger-Smith [Berlin: Nishen, n.d.], 14). For critical histories of still photography, film, and the liberation of the camps, see Janina Struk, *Photographing the Holocaust: Interpretations of the Evidence* (London: I. B. Tauris, 2004), 124–49; and Barbie Zelizer, ed., *Visual Culture and the Holocaust* (New Brunswick, N.J.: Rutgers University Press, 2001). For a discussion of the discursive history of the liberation of Belsen, see Joanne Reilly's tremendous study, *Belsen: The Liberation of a Concentration Camp* (London: Routledge, 1988).

5. I allude here to Lyotard's schematic presentation of the Kantian sublime as part of his elaboration of the distinction between the modern and the postmodern, both of which, he argues, partake of an aesthetics of the sublime, but only the latter of which achieves "the real sublime sentiment" (Jean-François Lyotard, *The Postmodern Condition*, trans. Geoff Bennington [Minneapolis: University of Minnesota Press, 1984], 81). This distinction quickly becomes complicated, as Lyotard goes on to define the postmodern not as an advancement over the modern, but rather as an emergent condition already at work within the modern, effectively splitting the modern within and against itself, leaving the postmodern to name the paradox whereby for a work to be "properly" modern, it must first betray the modern. In essence, the modern, like Lyotard's notion of the differend, presents a "case" (a work of art) that is unintelligible within the established norms of aesthetic judgment. I return to Lyotard's comments on the sublime below, but for the moment, it is important to note that Lyotard's narrative engages the challenge of thinking the postmodern sublime as part of the essay's critique of the conservative attack on the avant-garde or the political demand "to put an end to experimentation, in the arts and elsewhere," a demand subtended by the call for a "common way of speaking" (71).

6. Sontag, *On Photography*, 20. See also Geoffrey Gorer, "The Pornography of Death," *Encounter* 5, no. 4 (1955): 49–52.

7. See Philippe Ariès, *Western Attitudes toward Death*, trans. Patricia M. Ranum (Baltimore: Johns Hopkins University Press, 1974). According to Ariès, whereas death was once at the center of communal life, and whereas mourning rituals once functioned as sites of meaning and indicators of the

presence of meaning, in recent history, death has been multiply displaced, more and more subject to what Ariès calls the "death revolution," or an increasingly common "flight from death" (91). Thus death functions as a new yet unrecognized negativity, impossible to speak yet everywhere present—as symptom (of modernity, Americanization of culture, etc.). Ariès's narrative historicization of death confronts the inevitable problem of assuming the self-identity of its object—death—even as it claims to historicize the increasing (non)presence of this most phantom object, the most negative of things. Foucault takes on the limit-condition represented by death's place in the symbolic ("Power has no control over death"), historicizing the nonrecognition of individual death, as opposed to the regulation of species-life in the regularization of mortality, as an effect of the shifting investments of biopolitics. Michel Foucault, *Society Must Be Defended*, trans. David Macey (New York: Picador, 2003), 248.

8. Walter Benjamin, "The Work of Art in the Age of Mechanical Reproduction," in *Illuminations*, trans. Harry Zohn (New York: Schocken, 1968), 242; see also 250n19.

9. In my thinking about the driving, ideological pressure for a redemptive aesthetics, I am indebted to Leo Bersani's *The Culture of Redemption*. Bersani defines the "culture of redemption" as "a notion of art as making over or repairing failed experience" (*The Culture of Redemption* [Cambridge: Harvard University Press, 1990], 35).

10. The notion of atrocity tourism is not as fanciful or cynical as it might sound. It does, however, require precision. In his discussion of the history and dialectic of modern tourism, Hans Magnus Enzensberger demonstrates that beginning with its late eighteenth-century inception, the "ideology of tourism" is caught in the impasse of its own desire: The tourist wants to escape from bourgeois culture, but such an escape can take place only through and as extensions of bourgeois culture (extensions of the means of travel, such as the railroad, for instance). The problem of self-negation follows tourism wherever it goes, such that, the "pristine landscape and untouched history have remained the models of tourism. Tourism is nothing other than the attempt to realize the dream that Romanticism projected onto the distant and far away. To the degree that bourgeois society closed itself, the bourgeois tried to escape from it—as tourist. . . . [T]he network of the railroad system destroyed the very freedom it seemed to create: tourism had thought of the net as a liberation, but knitting this net every more tightly, society closed in again. . . . [T]ourism is always outrun by its refutation. This dialectic is the driving force of its very development." Enzensberger, "A Theory of Tourism," *New German Critique* 68 (1996): 125–26. If, as Enzensberger argues, tourism produces a desire for the always elsewhere, continuously projecting and enclosing the

frontier of space beyond, within this dialectic, the memorial spaces of the battlefield and the cemetery have long been coded to carry the weight of the sacred and pristine. As site of pilgrimage, the atrocity memorial or museum bears a similarly paradoxical burden. Enzensberger's essay, published in German in 1958, does not address the more recent iterations of the dialectic, in which the production of the pristine and the allure of the untouched remainder, along with the extended cult of the ruin, are supplemented by the desire to be touched by the historically significant remainder. Some critics, following a term coined by Malcolm Foley and John Lennon, have begun to carve out a discipline and discourse of "dark tourism." *Dark Tourism: The Attraction of Death and Disaster* (London: Continuum, 2000). Nonetheless, Enzensberger's essay remains powerful for its critical approach. As escape, he argues, tourism, "no matter how inane or helpless it may be, criticizes that from which it withdraws" (135).

11. See Theodor Adorno, "Commitment," in *Notes to Literature*, vol. 2, ed. Rolf Tiedemann, trans. Shierry Weber Nicholsen (New York: Columbia University Press, 1992). "I do not want to soften my statement that it is barbaric to continue to write poetry after Auschwitz. . . . It is the situation of literature itself and not simply one's relation to it that is paradoxical. . . . The so-called artistic rendering of the naked physical pain of those who were beaten down with rifle butts contains, however distantly, the possibility that pleasure can be squeezed from it. The morality that forbids art to forget this for a second slides off into the abyss of its opposite. The aesthetic stylistic principle, and even the chorus' solemn prayer, make the unthinkable appear to have had some meaning; it becomes transfigured, something of its horror removed" (87–88). The quotation that follows in the text is from page 89. For a discussion of Adorno's remarks on poetry after Auschwitz, see Michael Rothberg, *Traumatic Realism: The Demands of Holocaust Representation* (Minneapolis: University of Minnesota Press, 2000).

12. Georges Didi-Huberman, "Images Malgré Tout," in *Mémoire des Camps*, ed. Clément Chéroux (Paris: Éditions Marval, 2001), 219. In closing, Didi-Huberman returns to the impasse at work within an affirmation of the limit, or the negation of a negation, citing Beckett, "Nulle part trace de vie, dites-vous, pah, la belle affaire, imagination pas morte, si, bon, imagination morte imaginez" ("No trace anywhere of life, you say, pah, no difficulty there, imagination not dead yet, yes, dead, good, imagination dead imagine," from "Imagination Dead Imagine," in Samuel Beckett, *The Complete Short Prose* [New York: Grove, 1995], 182).

13. Hannah Arendt, *The Origins of Totalitarianism* (San Diego: Harvest, 1976), 444. For Arendt's arguments on the "banality of evil," see *Eichmann in Jerusalem* (New York: Penguin, 1994).

14. Raul Hilberg, in *The Destruction of the European Jews* (New York: Holmes and Meier, 1985), makes a case for the "precedents" already in place for the genocide, arguing that despite what "appears to us now as an unprecedented event in history," the events of the Holocaust were predicated on a long history such that "both perpetrators and victims drew upon their age-old experience in dealing with each other. The Germans did it with success. The Jews did it with disaster" (7, 24). Hilberg's appeal to historical precedent provides a counterargument against mystification (or appeals to the inexplicable), yet as he notes, many of the precedents he discusses were themselves incomplete and unfathomable within any prior framework or point of reference (12–13). Focusing specifically on the universe of terror that reigned in the camps, Wolfgang Sofsky makes a strong critique of comparative appeals to precedent, arguing that "although many structures of the camp picked up on historical models, the caesura in the history of power is unmistakable. The universe of the concentration camp is unprecedented in its torture and destruction" (*The Order of Terror*, trans. William Templer [Princeton: Princeton University Press, 1997], 279). The issues at stake here are legion (including the inevitable questions and displacements of retrospective judgment such as whether the victims ought to have anticipated, foreseen, prepared for, responded differently to the events). Such questions are inevitable because we want to believe that someone ought to have known (and as we now know, much more was known than was admitted—by the Allies in particular), and by implication that the outcome was not inevitable.

15. Immanuel Kant, *Critique of Judgment*, trans. Werner S. Pluhar (Indianapolis: Hackett, 1987), 110.

16. Ibid., 122.

17. See Slavoj Žižek, *The Puppet and the Dwarf* (Cambridge: MIT Press, 2003), 63; and *Welcome to the Desert of the Real* (London: Verso, 2002). Žižek takes the phrase the "passion for the real" from Alain Badiou. See Badiou, *The Century*, trans. Alberto Toscano (Cambridge, UK: Polity, 2007). Žižek's counterintuitive argument reverses the notion that we retreat into the safety of aesthetic form or narrative coherence in order to protect ourselves from an otherwise pressing threat of violence and disorder (such would be one way of reading Lyotard's critique of modernism—that version of the sublime that is also a shield *against* the sublime through the safety net of "proper form"). Rather, Žižek argues, it is the fantasy of such an other scene of actual or authentic violence that serves to protect us from the true threat or true horror—where the latter terms for Žižek usually translate, in a Lacanian vocabulary, as a species of fundamental impossibility. "Therein resides one of the fundamental lessons of psychoanalysis: the images of utter catastrophe, far from giving us access to the Real, can function as a protective shield AGAINST the real. In

sex as well as in politics, we take refuge in catastrophic scenarios in order to avoid the actual deadlock (of the impossibility of sexual relationship, of social antagonism)" (Slavoj Žižek, *The Art of the Ridiculous Sublime* [Seattle: University of Washington Press, 2002], 33–34).

18. G. L. Dickinson, *War* (London, 1923), cited in Modris Eksteins, *Rites of Spring* (Boston: Houghton Mifflin, 2000), 231–32.

19. Walter Benjamin, "The Storyteller," in *Illuminations*, trans. Harry Zohn (New York: Schocken, 1969), 84.

20. Eksteins, *Rites of Spring*, 228.

21. Sigmund Freud, "Thoughts for the Times on War and Death" [1915], in *The Standard Edition*, trans. James Strachey (London: Vintage, 2001), 14:291. Freud is at pains to stipulate that he speaks strictly of the experience of the bystanders, the noncombatants watching safely at a distance.

22. Ibid.

23. Ibid., 278–79.

24. Ibid., 281.

25. Maurice Blanchot, "The Apocalypse Is Disappointing," in *Friendship*, trans. Elizabeth Rottenberg (Stanford: Stanford University Press, 1997), 106.

26. Eric Hobsbawm, *The Age of Extremes* (New York: Vintage, 1996), 6–7.

27. Maurice Blanchot, *The Writing of the Disaster*, trans. Ann Smock (Lincoln: University of Nebraska Press, 1986), 51. The categories of the "disaster" and the "catastrophe" are not necessarily interchangeable. Particularly in Blanchot's work, where the figure of disaster is not easily stabilized or reduced to a concept, the translation between terms is restless at best. Still, one might follow Blanchot's questioning of the etymological, as he pushes the writing of disaster—as signifier and event—to the utmost tension, suspended between effective indeterminacy and the power of a vortex. "Naturally, 'disaster' can be understood according to its etymology—of which many fragments here bear the trace. But the etymology of 'disaster' does not operate in these fragments as a preferred, or more original insight, enduring mastery of what is no longer, then, anything but a word. On the contrary, the indeterminateness of what is written when this word is written, exceeds etymology and draws it into the disaster" (116–17).

28. Ibid., 9.

29. Alain Badiou, *Being and Event*, trans. Oliver Feltham (London: Continuum, 2005), 400.

30. Jean-Pierre Dupuy, *Petite Métaphysique des Tsunamis* (Paris: Éditions du Seuil, 2005); and *Pour un Catastrophisme Éclairé, Quand l'Impossible est Certain* (Paris: Éditions du Seuil, 2002).

31. Dupuy, *Petite Métaphysique des Tsunamis*, 18, translation mine.

32. Dupuy argues that in "the technological age, we do have an ardent obligation that we cannot fulfill: anticipating the future. That is the ethical

aporia" ("Rational Choice before the Apocalypse," available online at http://
politicaltheoryworkshop.googlepages.com/ApocalypticRatChoice.pdf).

33. Jean-François Lyotard, *The Postmodern Explained*, trans. Julian Pefanis
and Morgan Thomas (Minneapolis: University of Minnesota Press, 1993),
14–15.

34. Ibid., 15.

35. Jacques Derrida, "Phonographies: Meaning—from Heritage to Horizon," in *Echographies of Television*, with Bernard Stiegler, trans. Jennifer Ba-
jorek (Cambridge, UK: Polity, 2007), 105–6.

36. Ibid., 116.

37. How to think this very tension—the unprecedented as signifier of the
brink, language on the verge of the unsignifiable—without canceling its productive difficulties? How to make a case for the problem of the unprecedented
as historical preoccupation and formal impasse, when the case to be presented
includes, though it cannot include, the very question of thinking-presenting
the case without precedent? Yet of course there is precedent and one must
give examples. Hannah Arendt, noting the "chaos produced by the violence
of wars and revolutions and the growing decay of all that has still been
spared," gives voice to the dual accent of the unprecedented: Unprecedented
deracination threatens to undermine all grounds for meaning and stability;
generalized in a logic of "development" and the "same," the unprecedented
remains functionally descriptive of a historical condition. "Under the most
diverse conditions and disparate circumstances, we watch the development of
the same phenomena—homelessness on an unprecedented scale, rootlessness
to an unprecedented depth. Never has our future been more unpredictable,
never before" (*The Origins of Totalitarianism* [San Diego: Harvest, 1976], vii).

38. Ibid., 458. In holding out an ultimately irrepressible, non-negatable,
affirmative unpredictability as the essential characteristic of the human, and
therefore of human history, Arendt wants to challenge the lockdown on freedom and change that structures the totalitarian universe. Elsewhere, however,
when her argument leans on what she calls the "fact of natality," or the "mira-
cle that saves the world" (*The Human Condition* [Chicago: University of Chicago Press, 1998], 246–47), her logic of progressive futurity relies on an
idealized, abstracted normativity of reproductive life, a logic of generational
iterability that places all hope for the future in the symbolic beginning point
of birth, the figure of the child. For a critique of the rhetoric of futurism and
its fantasy of generational survival, coherence, and the desire for meaning in
the future, see Lee Edelman, *No Future: Queer Theory and the Death Drive*
(Durham, N.C.: Duke University Press, 2004).

39. Maurice Blanchot, *The Infinite Conversation*, trans. Susan Hanson (Minneapolis: University of Minnesota Press, 1993), 275.

40. Immanuel Kant, "What Is Enlightenment?" in *Perpetual Peace and Other Essays*, trans. Ted Humphrey (Indianapolis: Hackett, 1983), 43–44.

41. Hans Jonas, *The Imperative of Responsibility: In Search of an Ethics for the Technological Age*, trans. Hans Jonas and David Herr (Chicago: University of Chicago Press, 1984), 37, 43, 22.

42. Reinhart Koselleck, "Progress and Decline," in *The Practice of Conceptual History*, trans. Todd Samuel Presner et al. (Stanford: Stanford University Press, 2002), 233.

43. Avital Ronell, *The Telephone Book* (Lincoln: University of Nebraska Press, 1989), 16.

44. "Catastrophe," *Oxford English Dictionary*.

45. Gustav Freytag, *Freytag's Technique of the Drama* (Chicago: Scott, Foresman, 1900), 137–38.

46. Jonas, *The Imperative of Responsibility*, 127–28.

47. Karl Marx and Friedrich Engels, *The Communist Manifesto* (New York: International Publishers, 1994), 12.

48. Ibid. The tension in this passage turns on its troping of material states: solid, liquid, gas. On the one hand, Marx emphasizes the disappearing of the solid, and on the other, he puts forward the grounds for a new, and newly revolutionary, approach to the "real conditions of life." Perhaps the most interesting moment in Marx's crossing of this aporia—there is no ground, let me speak to you of (and from) the new ground—is the condition and interpretation of liquidity. If, in the physical sciences, sublimation is defined as the skipping of states, as in the case of a solid's bypassing liquidity and becoming a gas, Marx's formulation loosely implies such a shift in material state—the solid becomes dispersed not, strictly speaking, into "gas" but "air"—and yet at the same time the verb "melts" introduces the trope of the liquid state. For a discussion of the tropes of liquidity and speed, see Paul Virilio, *Crepuscular Dawn*, trans. Mike Taormina (New York: Semiotext(e), 2002). For a discussion of the underlying threat of uncertainty in the discourses of globalization, where the dangers of the liquid form are associated with contamination, leakage, and the porosity of borders, see Zygmunt Bauman, *Liquid Times: Living in an Age of Uncertainty* (Cambridge, UK: Polity, 2007).

49. Joseph Conrad's *Heart of Darkness* has become, perhaps, the exemplary text for reading such an image. Although the novel historicizes the envisioning of "blank spaces on the earth," signaling its end in the form of Africa's becoming "filled up" (11–12), the language and structure of Conrad's narrative problematizes, obsessively and without resolution, what it means to assert, and for that matter to challenge, the governing oppositions between the blank and the named, the primitive and the civilized, nature and language, prehistory and history. Joseph Conrad, *Heart of Darkness* (New York: Norton, 1988).

50. Peter Bürger, *Theory of the Avant-Garde*, trans. Michael Shaw (Minneapolis: University of Minnesota Press, 1987).

51. "All distances in time and space are shrinking," and yet, "the frantic abolition of all distances brings no nearness; for nearness does not consist in shortness of distance" (Martin Heidegger, "The Thing," in *Poetry, Language, Thought*, trans. Albert Hofstadter [New York: Harper and Row, 1971], 165). For Heidegger, the "domination of the distanceless" (181) serves only to make nearness all the less presentable, all the more remote.

52. Karl Marx, *Grundrisse*, trans. Martin Nicolaus (London: Penguin, 1973), 408, 524, 539.

53. Virginia Woolf, "Mr. Bennett and Mrs. Brown," in *The Captain's Death Bed and Other Essays* (San Diego: Harvest, 1978), 96.

54. H. J. Mackinder, "The Geographical Pivot of History," *Geographical Journal* 23, no. 4 (1904): 421–37.

55. Benton Mackaye, "Industrial Exploration," *Nation*, July 27, 1927.

56. Ibid.

57. Rudyard Kipling, "Some Aspects of Travel," in *The Collected Works of Rudyard Kipling* (Garden City, N.Y.: Doubleday, 1941), 24:91–107. Kipling's discussion of visualization—he uses phrases such as "our mental pictures of travel" and the "mind-picture" (97)—situates the image between the Imaginary and the Symbolic. On the one hand, it is as if the "mind-picture" takes place without being spoken or externalized in language (thus Kipling becomes a kind of seer and intruder, a mind-picture-thief). On the other, his approach to "mental atlases" and "mental sign-talk" acknowledges the mental-visual as graphic and available only as *read*. What is important here is that Kipling presupposes and projects a universal singular—the traveler he speaks of is presumed as representative of "all." For example, when speaking of the foreshortening of the "way-signal" or "time-conception" of the voyage (by these terms Kipling implies something like the historical general equivalent for thinking "how long from point A to point B," where "length" is measured both as time and lines in space), he speaks of "that indescribable diagram of time which rises in each man's mind at the mention of a voyage of known length," and concludes that in the coming years this "indescribable diagram," its resistance to description notwithstanding, "will be shrunk to a little block or bead or shadow representing forty-eight or fifty hours. And so it will be with all voyages" (98).

58. Ibid., 91; emphasis added.

59. For a discussion of the cartographic imagination and the colonial discourse of information control, see Thomas Richards, *The Imperial Archive: Knowledge and the Fantasy of Empire* (London: Verso, 1993).

60. Kipling, "Some Aspects of Travel," 106.

61. For a discussion of the "nuclear event" and the "remainderless destruction," see Jacques Derrida, "No Apocalypse, Not Now (Full Speed Ahead, Seven Missiles, Seven Missives)," *Diacritics* 14 (Summer 1984): 21–31.

62. Victor Segalen, *Essay on Exoticism: An Aesthetics of Diversity*, trans. Yaël Rachel Schlick (Durham, N.C.: Duke University Press, 2002). Erich Auerbach's essay is the concluding chapter to his *Mimesis: The Representation of Reality in Western Literature*, trans. Willard R. Trask (Princeton: Princeton University Press, 1953).

63. Auerbach, *Mimesis*, 538. When Auerbach argues that in "Virginia Woolf's case the exterior events have actually lost their hegemony" (538), one might note in the accent on such loss some of the essay's ambivalence and uncertainty over what some have called modernism's subjective turn, or what Auerbach describes as a turn toward interiority and the writing of the thought-event. As I argue above, Auerbach's representation of modernism is structured by dialectics of exteriority and interiority, objective determination and subjective universality, historical inheritance and revolutionary change, discontinuity and commonality. The conflict that runs throughout is not only between these paired oppositions but also over the political implications of their movement, which Auerbach suggests echoes the tendential proximity between factionalism and fascism (550). As for the outlook on the future, Auerbach ends the essay noting a new, and perhaps final, historical synthesis that forebodes the end of difference (553).

64. Ibid., 549. Recent criticism has taken note of significant peculiarities in the work as a whole, in part by attending to the text's investment in and displacement of the category of the "whole" as a formal, ideological, methodological problem (for instance, the question of the text's framing of "Western literature" as a whole; or of Auerbach's "representation" of the "Representation of Realism" as comprehensive survey). As Auerbach's states in his epilogue, the work itself owes its existence and its method to the alienating, antisystematic, decentering conditions under which it was written. At the same time, Edward Said and others have argued, the effects of exile, Auerbach's in Istanbul during the Second World War included, are hardly interesting if they serve merely to reaffirm, typically with a longing for the threatened first term, the hierarchical oppositions between center and margin, inside and outside, Europe and its others, sanctified past and disenchanted present. See Edward Said, *The World, the Text, and the Critic* (Cambridge: Harvard University Press, 1983), 21; and Aamir Mufti, "Auerbach in Istanbul," *Critical Inquiry* 25 (Autumn 1998): 95–125. For a discussion of the modernism of Auerbach's text, and of its historicism in particular, see Hayden White, "Auerbach's Literary History," in *Figural Realism* (Baltimore: Johns Hopkins University Press, 1999), 87–100.

65. Auerbach, *Mimesis*, 552.

2. VIRGINIA WOOLF: READING REMAINS

1. In "Perpetual Peace," Kant anticipates the apocalyptic breach that threatens to make war not only a repeated historical event but rather a "war to end all." Kant's negative scenario requires none of the twentieth century's advanced means of destruction to make its case. Instead, Kant focuses on the threat that certain "dishonourable stratagems," were they to be normalized within the practices of war, should inevitably lead to a terminal escalation of hostilities, or the "vast graveyard of humanity as a whole" induced by a "war of extermination." "Some level of trust in the enemy's way of thinking [*Denkungsart*] must be preserved even in the midst of war, for otherwise no peace can ever be concluded and the hostilities would become a war of extermination (*bellum internecinum*). . . . From this it follows that a war of extermination— where the destruction of both parties along with all rights as a result—would permit perpetual peace to occur only in the vast graveyard of humanity as a whole. Thus, such a war, including all means used to wage it, must be absolutely prohibited" (Immanuel Kant, "Perpetual Peace," in *Perpetual Peace and Other Essays*, trans. Ted Humphrey [Indianapolis: Hackett, 1983], 109–10).

2. *Beyond the Visible: The Art of Odilon Redon*, ed. Jodi Hauptman (New York: Museum of Modern Art, 2005), 118–19. Redon's Eye-Balloon is a memento mori for the species. Redon made two versions of the image, the first a charcoal drawing in 1878, the second the lithograph, for his portfolio, *To Edgar Poe*, in 1882. I have included the later image.

3. Immanuel Kant, "Perpetual Peace," 110.

4. The 1868 St. Petersburg Declaration seeks to maintain a fantasy in which the "civilized nations" might still, and indeed for the future, exercise sovereignty over the meaning and definition of humanity in the practice of war. Established "in order to examine the expediency of forbidding the use of certain projectiles in time of war between civilized nations, and that Commission having by common agreement fixed the technical limits at which the necessities of war ought to yield to the requirements of humanity," the 1868 Declaration launches a discourse organized around the newly charged gravity of the "projectile," a figure for the nascent, though still unmentioned, technologies of aerial warfare. With the 1899 Hague Declaration on the Launching of Projectiles and Explosives from Balloons, and again in the revisions of the 1907 Hague International Peace Conference, technologies of flight make their first official appearance in the quasi-legal register of international law. It is not until 1922 that a post–balloon discourse aimed at restricting the future of aerial warfare begins to take shape. For the language of the St. Petersburg Declaration, as well as that of the 1899 Declaration (which, as part of the 1899 Final Act of the International Peace Conference at the Hague, is guided by

the resolution, "The Conference is of the opinion that the restriction of military charges, which are at present a heavy burden on the world, is extremely desirable for the increase of the material and moral welfare of mankind"), and the 1907 revisions, see http://www.icrc.org/ihl.nsf/INTRO/130?OpenDocument; and http://www.icrc.org/ihl.nsf/INTRO/160?OpenDocument; and http://www.icrc.org/ihl.nsf/FULL/245?OpenDocument; and for the 1922 document, "Rules Concerning the Control of Wireless Telegraphy in the Time of War and Air Warfare," see http://www.icrc.org/ihl.nsf/FULL/275?OpenDocument.

5. H. G. Wells, *The War That Will End War* (New York: Duffield, 1914), 12.

6. Max Horkheimer and Theodor Adorno, *Dialectic of Enlightenment*, trans. Edmund Jephcott (Stanford: Stanford University Press, 2002), 186.

7. G. B. Shaw, "Common Sense about the War," *New Statesman*, supplement, November 14, 1914.

8. H. G. Wells, *The Last War: A World Set Free* (Lincoln: University of Nebraska Press, 2001), 60–61.

9. H. G. Wells, *Discovery of the Future* [1903] (London: Jonathan Cape, 1913).

10. H. G. Wells, "Forecasting the Future," in *What Is Coming? A European Forecast* (New York: Macmillan, 1917), 1.

11. Lord Montagu of Beaulieu, *Aerial Machines and War* (London: Hugh Rees, 1910), 2.

12. Ibid., 10.

13. Indeed, Montagu consistently refers to the past in order to justify his speculations about the future. Thus the future "corps of areoplanists" will reproduce the model of the cavalry (ibid., 6); as in the past, the rule of "meeting like with like" will hold, such that the "theory of meeting the enemy with his own weapon has been proved to be correct over and over again in history, and will be proved correct many more times" (9).

14. Ibid., 8.

15. Inevitable and irreversible, entropy is a law that insists on increasing indifference, a universe in which the totality of energy (an originary, fixed, and finite universe of free energy or neg-entropy) that remains available for future, different, and new moves is always decreasing. Thus the Second Law of Thermodynamics can be understood as a twisted version of a Hegelian "last" negation, where Absolute Spirit realizes itself only at the moment when there is no more remainder to do the work of synthesis, in other words, "after" the end of the world. The *Augenblick* of entropy is consummately blind. For Marx, however, the point is precisely not to see the universe from the point of view of an apocalyptic, absolute terminus but rather to harness the forces of history

toward directed (perhaps even auto-directed) ends in the now. The quotation on entropy and melting is from Rosalind Krauss and Yve-Alain Bois, "A User's Guide to Entropy" (*October* 78 [Fall 1996]: 53), and is useful for calling attention to the troping of entropy as law. One might anticipate a marxian critique of a "vulgar physics," aimed at models of history for which entropy would function as reductive, explanatory rule, an explanation that would perhaps serve to naturalize and normalize the universal melting effect, or the all-encompassing spread of disorder (that tends, paradoxically, toward the homogenizing, leveling effect, the cumulative "order" called entropy). For a critical reading of the "metaphysics" of entropy, see Henri Bergson, *Creative Evolution*, trans. Arthur Mitchell (Mineola, N.Y.: Dover Publications, 1988), 243.

16. Edward Said, "A Note on Modernism," in *Culture and Imperialism* (New York: Vintage, 1994), 189.

17. Ibid.

18. Georg Lukács. "The Ideology of Modernism," in *Realism in Our Time: Literature and the Class Struggle*, trans. John Mander and Necke Mander (New York: Harper and Row, 1962), 17–46.

19. Virginia Woolf, "The Fascination of the Pool," in *The Complete Shorter Fiction of Virginia Woolf* (San Diego: Harvest, 1989), 226.

20. Ibid.

21. In "Autobiography as De-Facement," Paul de Man defines prosopopeia as "the fiction of the voice-from-beyond-the grave" (*The Rhetoric of Romanticism* [New York: Columbia University Press, 1984], 77). De Man's formulation of prosopopeia emerges in a discussion of autobiography as epitaphic discourse but extends to any text in which the inscribed "I" would represent the speaker in his or her absence, across the thresholds of death, disappearance, silence, and even publication. Thus, while de Man begins his reading of autobiography with Wordsworth's *Essays upon Epitaphs*, he extends it to "any book with a readable title page" (70).

22. Virginia Woolf, *A Room of One's Own* (San Diego: Harvest, 1929), 89.

23. Virginia Woolf, *Three Guineas* (San Diego: Harvest, 1938), 75.

24. Woolf, *A Room of One's Own*, 89. Woolf's fascination with figures of remainder, negation, and dispersal can be found in a range of her texts. The phrase "what remains" appears in "Women and Fiction" (a previously published version of the Cambridge lectures that became *A Room of One's Own*), where Woolf sets the gendering of the remainder in stark relief when she asks, "But of our mothers, our grandmothers, our great-grandmothers, what remains?" (76). Her fiction displays a similar concern with the language of "what remains" as it engages the limits of history, biography, and empiricism. In *Jacob's Room*, as the narrator attempts to describe Jacob, the phrase is invoked as a way of marking an impossibility: "But though all this may very well be

true . . . there remains over something which can never be conveyed . . . what remains is mostly a matter of guesswork" (*Jacob's Room* [San Diego: Harvest, 1922], 72–73). And in *Orlando*, the narrator interrogates the limits of life-writing with the question, "But what, the reader may ask with some exasperation, happened in between? . . . And of it all, what remains?" (*Orlando* [San Diego: Harvest, 1928], 199).

25. Walter Benjamin, "On the Mimetic Faculty," in *Selected Writings, Volume 2: 1927–1934* (Cambridge: Harvard University Press, 1999), 722.

26. Virginia Woolf, "On Not Knowing Greek," in *The Common Reader* (San Diego: Harvest, 1984), 23. The quotation to follow is from the same page.

27. I intentionally recall with the violation of a reversal P. B. Shelley's phrasing of poetry as that which "compels us to feel that which we perceive, and to imagine that which we know" (Percy Bysshe Shelley, "A Defence of Poetry," in *Shelley's Poetry and Prose*, ed. Donald Reiman [New York: Norton, 1977], 505).

28. Woolf, "On Not Knowing Greek," 23.

29. Ibid., 27; emphasis added.

30. Ibid., 24.

31. The critique of the urban and its polluting, necrological effects becomes the driving force of England's garden city movement. See, for instance, Ebenezer Howard, who writes that London must change or "London must die" (*Garden Cities of To-morrow* [London: Swan, 1902], 147).

32. Woolf, "On Not Knowing Greek," 35.

33. Ibid., 34.

34. Ibid., 38.

35. All references to Virginia Woolf, *To the Lighthouse* (1927; San Diego: Harvest, 1981) will be made parenthetically within the text.

36. Lukács, "The Ideology of Modernism," 32–35.

37. Fredric Jameson, *A Singular Modernity: Essay on the Ontology of the Present* (London: Verso, 2002).

38. Virginia Woolf, "Mr. Bennett and Mrs. Brown," in *The Captain's Death Bed and Other Essays* (San Diego: Harvest, 1978), 103.

39. In "Modern Fiction," Woolf makes an appeal for such an attunement as part of her attempt to distinguish the specific accent of the modern. "From all sides they come, an incessant shower of innumerable atoms; and as they fall, as they shape themselves into the life of Monday or Tuesday, the accent falls differently from old; the moment of importance came not here but there. . . . Let us record the atoms as they fall upon the mind in the order in which they fall, let us trace the pattern, however disconnected and incoherent in appearance, which each sight or incident scores upon the consciousness.

Let us not take it for granted that life exists more fully in what is commonly thought big than in what is commonly thought small" (Virginia Woolf, "Modern Fiction," in *The Common Reader*, 150).

40. Virginia Woolf, *Mrs. Dalloway* (San Diego: Harvest, 1981), 8.

41. Virginia Woolf, "How It Strikes a Contemporary," in *The Common Reader* (San Diego: Harvest, 1984), 234. The passages that follow are from 232 and 233.

42. Ibid., 237.

43. In her reading of "Time Passes," Karen L. Levenback argues that Woolf emplaces the idiom of war in the voice of a narrator who remains clueless about its meaning and about the war altogether. "[N]otwithstanding the increased frequency of the military imaging . . . the narrator seems to have no clue as to its context." Calling on us not "to miss the crucial point Woolf is making about the lack of consciousness," Levenback finds a fullness of authorial consciousness precisely where the narrator's (and reader's) may fall short. More specifically, Levenback ascribes to the narrator's lack of consciousness a representative yet self-critical function (the relationship between the two is not quite clear), arguing it speaks for the limited scope and authority of the civilian point of view. "Such metaphors . . . invite the reader to question the authority of the civilian point of view represented by the narrator" (Karen L. Levenback, *Virginia Woolf and the Great War* [Syracuse: Syracuse University Press, 1999], 104). Although I remain indebted to Levenback's detailed research, and particularly to her reading of the effects of the General Strike in May 1926 on Woolf as she wrote *To the Lighthouse*, I am not convinced by her reading of "Time Passes," which remains caught in the deadlocked oppositions that have long troubled modernist criticism as it tries to hold literature above, yet at the same time accountable to, a fantasy of a grounded, ground-leveled, untroubled presentation of history.

44. For a reading of the "interwar," the rhetoric of anticipation, and the writing of war in the air, see Paul K. Saint-Amour, "Air War Prophecy and Interwar Modernism," *Comparative Literature Studies* 42, no. 2 (2005), 130–61.

45. Some critics have charged modernism with complicity in a larger social disavowal of the war and its dead. Margot Norris reads modernism's "suppression of the war dead" through "its suppression of trench poetry" (as evinced in Yeats's 1936 rejection of the so-called trench poets from *The Oxford Book of Modern Verse*). I think Norris overstates modernism's formal and ideological aspirations, not to mention its internal coherence and distinct identity. The idea that modernism's formal strategies can be read as a response to the war (even an anticipatory one) is certainly neither controversial nor new, but Norris takes the case further; repeating a by now traditional critique of high-modernism, Norris argues that modernism turns toward antirepresentational

formalism so as to eclipse a series of burgeoning threats: mass warfare, mass death, and mass culture. "By destroying artists, the war destroyed art and reproduced the operation of mass culture in the voluminous, indiscriminate production of its dead. Modernism responded by replacing representation with performance—both in textual strategy and in institutional practice" (Margot Norris, *Writing War in the Twentieth Century* [Charlottesville: University Press of Virginia, 2000], 36).

46. See Norris, *Writing War in the Twentieth Century*, 37.

47. Longinus, "On Sublimity," in *Ancient Literary Criticism*, ed. D. A. Russell and M. Winterbottom (Oxford: Oxford University Press, 1972), 482–83.

48. Ibid., 496, 495.

3. WALTER BENJAMIN ON RADIO: CATASTROPHE FOR CHILDREN

1. "Modernity must stand under the sign of suicide, an act which seals a heroic will that makes no concessions to a mentality inimical toward this will. Such a suicide is not a resignation but heroic passion. It is *the* achievement of modernity in the realm of the passions" (Walter Benjamin, "The Paris of the Second Empire in Baudelaire," in *Selected Writings, Volume 4: 1938–1940* [Cambridge: Harvard University Press, 2003], 45). One among several of Benjamin's comments on suicide (as with so much of his work, if one strings them together, they will not add up), the argument here wants to read "heroic suicide" as part of a newly meaningful—modern—aesthetics of destruction and politics of violence.

2. Among their many photographic traces, both authors are photographed by Gisèle Freund in the two years before their deaths. Freund's famous closeup of Benjamin is taken in 1938 (reproduced in Momme Brodersen, *Walter Benjamin: A Biography*, trans. Malcolm R. Green and Ingrida Ligers [London: Verso, 1996], 243). Woolf's June 1939 session with Freund, whom Woolf refers to as that "devil woman," produced a series of portraits that are, to my mind, fascinating precisely because they are so painfully inscrutable and blank. In them, Woolf's face, and in some cases her stare, withdraws into a paradoxical inexpressivity for which interpretive readings of expressive content—the notion that they express or represent Woolf's exhaustion, irritation, refusal, boredom, or other condition of affective interiority—become utterly tenuous. For a discussion of Woolf as multivalent icon, see Brenda R. Silver, *Virginia Woolf: Icon* (Chicago: University of Chicago Press, 1999), with reproductions of some of Freund's images on pages 18 and 19. (Not provided in Silver is the most drastically ambivalent of the Freund photographs, an image in which the sharpness of Woolf's gaze is both direct and withholding, interrupting any sense of pathos or identificatory longing; it can be found in Maggie Humm, *Snapshots of Bloomsbury: The Private Lives of Virginia Woolf and Vanessa Bell*

[New Brunswick, N.J.: Rutgers University Press, 2006], 165.) Benjamin's ico-
nicity, disseminated widely throughout a range of disciplines and across the
spectrum of critical culture (perhaps as a founding name for that most dispersed of terms, "critical theory") remains incommensurate with that of
Woolf, as the latter, if only in name, has reached into the realm of a more
recognizably popular appropriation. In his *Icons of the Left: Benjamin and Eise-
nstein, Picasso and Kafka after the Fall of Communism* (Chicago: University of
Chicago Press, 1999), Otto Karl Werckmeister reads the desire invested in the
icon as a symptom of a politically reactive, historically blind "Marxist culture
of capitalism" (5). Werckmeister's arguments for historical specificity are ag-
gressively simplistic. In a dismissal of a culture of "left-wing intellectuals" and
academics who, Werckmeister insists, fail to recognize the truth of their own
moribund desire, Werckmeister criticizes, for instance, all those readers of
Benjamin (he does not name them) for whom, "The Angel of History has
become a symbolic figure for the contradiction-laden alignment of life, art,
and politics to which left-wing academics have aspired, an alignment that in
turn fascinates left-wing academics emulating such aspirations" (12). Having
posited such a generic critical tendency and structure of desire, he goes on to
attack those critics who "posit a seemingly absolute subject, detached from
Benjamin's historical situation in 1940" (12). When otherwise engaged, Werckmeister's text can be compelling.

   3. For Blanchot's comments on suicide, see *The Space of Literature*, trans.
Ann Smock (Lincoln: The University of Nebraska Press, 1982), esp. 95–107.
For Žižek's discussion of the difference between the "suicide '*in* reality,'"
which "remains caught in the network of symbolic communication," and the
radical act constituted through "symbolic suicide," see Slavoj Žižek, *Enjoy Your
Symptom! Jacques Lacan in Hollywood and Out* (Routledge: New York: 1992),
43–44. Whereas Žižek critiques suicide as an essentially failed and miscon-
strued attempt to cheat death of its negativity, Blanchot's discussion, even as
it allows that the suicide, like the artist, "succeed[s] in doing something only
by deceiving themselves about what they do" (106), takes less interest in diag-
nosing the false or misrecognized desire of suicide, or what for Žižek amounts
to the suicide's desire to hold onto meaning as and through self-sacrifice.
Rather, for Blanchot, it is in assuming the impossibility of suicide, its desire
for sovereign execution and the death-mastering (or even death-defying)
event, that the difficulty begins.

   4. Much of Benjamin's work on radio remains untranslated. The radio
work for children, the extant manuscripts of which are gathered together as
Rundfunkgeschichten für Kinder, can be found in Benjamin, *Gesammelte Schriften*, vol. 7.1, ed. Rolf Tiedemann and Hermann Schweppenhäuser (Frankfurt:
Suhrkamp Verlag, 1989), 68–249, with notes in *GS*, vol. 7.2, 582–616. For the

Hörmodelle, see *GS*, vol. 4.2, ed. Tillman Rexroth (Frankfurt: Suhrkamp Verlag, 1972), 627–720, with notes at 1053–73. See also the texts gathered as *Literarische Rundfunkvorträge* in *GS*, vol. 7.1, ed. Rolf Tiedemann and Hermann Schweppenhäuser (Frankfurt: Suhrkamp Verlag, 1989), 251–94, with notes in vol. 7.2, 608–34, where the editors provide locations for related material. For the most comprehensive study of Benjamin's radio works to date, see Sabine Schiller-Lerg, *Walter Benjamin und der Rundfunk: Programmarbeit zwischen Theorie und Praxis* (Munich: K. G. Saur, 1984). For a condensed plot of Benjamin's work on radio, see Momme Brodersen, *Walter Benjamin: A Biography*, trans. Malcolm R. Green and Ingrida Ligers (London: Verso, 1996), 191–94. See also "Sabine Schiller-Lerg, "Walter Benjamin, Radio Journalist: Theory and Practice of Weimar Radio," trans. Susan Nieschlag, *Journal of Communication Inquiry* 13, no. 1 (1989): 43–50.

5. See Walter Benjamin, "Two Types of Popularity: Fundamental Reflections on a Radio Play," in *The Work of Art in the Age of Its Technological Reproducibility and Other Writings on Media*, ed. Michael W. Jennings et al., trans. Edmund Jephcott et al. (Cambridge: Harvard University Press, 2008), 403–6.

6. Walter Benjamin, "Children's Literature" [1929], in *Selected Writings, Volume 2: 1927–1934*, trans. Rodney Livingstone et al. (Cambridge: Harvard University Press, 1999), 252.

7. In the correspondence, Benjamin's references to his work for radio are nearly always delivered in the context of financial concerns, anxiety over which only increases in the years leading up to his departure in March 1933. For the remarks to Scholem quoted in the text, see Gershom Scholem, *Walter Benjamin: The Story of a Friendship*, trans. Harry Zohn (New York: New York Review Books, 1981), 211; and *The Correspondence of Walter Benjamin, 1910–1940*, ed. Gershom Scholem and Theodor W. Adorno, trans. Manfred R. Jacobson and Evelyn M. Jacobson (Chicago: University of Chicago Press, 1994), 404, with Scholem's footnote, 404n12.

8. For the structure and distribution of power in Weimar radio, see Karl Christian Führer, "A Medium of Modernity? Broadcasting in Weimar Germany, 1923–1932," *Journal of Modern History* 69 (December 1997): 722–53. See also Mark E. Cory, "Soundplay: The Polyphonous Tradition of German Radio Art," in *Wireless Imagination: Sound, Radio, and the Avant-Garde*, ed. Douglas Kahn and Gregory Whitehead (Cambridge: MIT Press, 1992), 331–71. Cory's piece provides an excellent discussion of the history of the *Hörspiel* as it emerged after the Second World War, with particular focus on attempts to wrest radio art from the conventions of "traditionally literary, that is, semantically organized" narrative (354), or to open the way for the "soundplay" of experimental acoustics.

9. Douglas Kahn, "Introduction: Histories of Sound Once Removed," in *Wireless Imagination; Sound, Radio, and the Avant-Garde*, ed. Douglas Kahn and Gregory Whitehead (Cambridge: MIT Press, 1992), 2.

10. For a discussion of the historical invention of "liveness," see Philip Auslander, *Liveness: Performance in a Mediatized Culture* (London: Routledge, 1999). Auslander argues that the idiom and aura of the live event come into being only with the recent history of technologies of reproduction and, moreover, only after "the maturation of mediatized society" (58). The latter distinction is important to Auslander's understanding of the gap between developments in sound recording in the late nineteenth century (in particular the gramophone) and the emergence of the word "live," which appears only in 1934, and which Auslander suggests is an effect of radio, which, curiously (given that the distinction is ostensibly not yet in play), "put the clear opposition of the live and the recorded into a state of crisis" (59).

11. For an early articulation of the phonautograph, a device that anticipates the well-known moment in *Ulysses* during which Bloom imagines a gramophone that, as reproduced and reproducible sound recording, would extend the afterlife of the dead as encrypted yet rehearable voice ("Remind you of the voice like the photograph reminds you of the face" (James Joyce, *Ulysses* [New York: Vintage, 1986], 6.962–63, p. 93), see Emile Berliner, "The Gramophone: Etching the Human Voice," *Journal of the Franklin Institute* 125, no. 6 (June 1888): 425–506. "Future generations will be able to condense within the space of twenty minutes a tone picture of a single lifetime. Five minutes of the child's prattle, five of the boy's exultations, five of the man's reflections, and five of the feeble utterances from the death-bed. Will it not be like holding communion even with immortality?" (Berliner, 446).

12. On the "notoriously fragile and difficult to hear" traces of early radio and its rarefied incunabula, see Jonathan Sterne, *The Audible Past: Cultural Origins of Sound Reproduction* (Durham, N.C.: Duke University Press, 2003), 288. Commenting on "the disjuncture between the imagination and the practice of early phonography," Sterne argues, "Writers imagined that the technology finally set free the voices of the dead, but this permanence in the technology or the medium was more imagined than real. If anything, permanence was less a description of the power of the medium than a program for its development. . . . [D]eath is everywhere among the living in early discussions of sound's reproducibility" (288–89).

13. Eduardo Cadava, *Words of Light: Theses on the Photography of History* (Princeton: Princeton University Press, 1997), 130.

14. Walter Benjamin, "Theses on the Philosophy of History," in *Illuminations*, trans. Harry Zohn (New York: Schocken, 1968), 257–58.

15. Ibid., 257.

16. Walter Benjamin, "Geschichtsphilosophische Thesen," in *Illuminationen* (Frankfurt am Main: Suhrkamp Verlag, 1961), 272–73.

17. For a critique of the "consolatory" and "melancholic" view of Benjamin's angel, see Giorgio Agamben, "Walter Benjamin and the Demonic: Happiness and Historical Redemption," in *Potentialities*, trans. Daniel Heller-Roazen (Stanford: Stanford University Press, 1999), 138–59.

18. The four lines of the poem as excerpted in the epigraph read, "My wing is ready for flight, I would like to turn back. If I stayed timeless time, I would have little luck [Mein Flügel ist zum Schwung bereit,/ich kehrte gern zurück, /denn blieb ich auch lebendige Zeit, /ich hätte wenig Glück]" (*Illuminations*, 257). For an alternative translation, see *Selected Writings, Volume 4*, 392.

19. Walter Benjamin, "The Railway Disaster at the Firth of Tay," in *Selected Writings, Volume 2*, 564. Hereafter cited parenthetically in the text. The German here is instructive, as it draws attention to Benjamin's language of beginnings, evident as he attempts to trace technology in its initial uptake. "Seht ihr nun, was ich meinte, als ich sagte, dass die Leute damals eigentlich noch nicht recht wussten, was sie mit der Technik anfangen sollten" ("Die Eisenbahnkatastrophe vom Firth of Tay," in *Gesammelte Schriften*, vol. 7.1, 233). For the history of this broadcast, which aired over Berlin radio on February 4, 1932, and over Frankfurt radio on March 30, 1932 (*Gesammelte Schriften*, vol. 7.2, 605), and was delivered as part of Benjamin's participation in radio programming for children, see Jeffrey Mehlman, *Walter Benjamin for Children: An Essay on His Radio Years* (Chicago: University of Chicago Press, 1993).

20. On the aesthetics of war and the fantasy of species annihilation, see the concluding paragraph of "The Work of Art in the Age of Mechanical Reproduction," where Benjamin argues, "Its [mankind's] self-alienation has reached such a degree that it can experience its own destruction as an aesthetic pleasure of the first order" (*Illuminations*, 242, and *Selected Writings, Volume 4*, which offers a slightly different translation [270].)

21. See "Reflections on Radio," and "Theater and Radio," in *Selected Writings, Volume 2*, 543–44 and 583–86.

22. The figures Benjamin uses in these texts for the fall or downturn or destructive work of catastrophe are variable. He interchanges catastrophe (*Katastrophe*); misfortune, mishap, disaster (*Unglück*); (down)fall (*Untergang*). Variations on the negative—violence, loss, destruction, annihilation, disappearance, undoing, and death—are frequent. A common thread is a note of fright, terror, shock (*Schrecken, schrecklich*) and horror (*Graus*). Here the passage reads, "Von Eisenbahnunglück erzähl' ich euch heute. Aber nicht nur so als Schrecken und Graus, sondern ich will es in die Geschichte der Technik, besonders in die des Eisenbaus hineinstellen. Es ist da von einer Brücke die Rede. Diese Brücke stürzt ein. Gewiß ist das schrecklich für die 200 Menschen, die dabei ums Leben kamen, für ihre Angehörigen und viele andere.

Aber doch will ich euch dieses Unglück darstellen nur wie einen kleinen Zwischenfall in einem großen Kampfe, in dem die Menschen siegreich geblieben sind und siegreich bleiben werden, wenn sie nicht etwa selbst ihre Arbeit wieder vernichten" (Benjamin, *Gesammelte Schriften*, vol. 7.1, 232).

23. The passage repeats a citation, here unmarked as such, which appears, with slight variations, elsewhere in Benjamin's work: In "The Ring of Saturn or Some Remarks on Iron Construction," where it is attributed to "the first historian of iron construction" (*The Arcades Project*, trans. Howard Eiland and Kevin McLaughlin (Cambridge: Harvard University Press, 1999), 887. (This draft text, in which Benjamin refers to the story of the Firth of Tay, presents an early montage of the interests that will reappear in the 1932 radio broadcast.) The passage also appears in *The Arcades Project*'s section "Iron Construction" (Convolute F, pp.160–61 [F4a, 2]), where Benjamin attributes by name, citing A. G. Meyer's *Eisenbauten*, a work on which Benjamin relies heavily throughout this section of the *Project*. See A. G. Meyer, *Eisenbauten* (Esslingen: Paul Neff, 1907).

24. Radio begins to take over from wireless telegraphy at the end of the nineteenth century but does not carry as clearly the latter term's sense of subtraction, or the "less"-ness, that designates telegraphy's transmission across distance without the use of wires or cables. The emphasis on a dematerialized path is picked up and heightened by telepathy, which transmits something like feeling, pain, or thought "through empty space without employing the familiar methods of communication by words and signs" (Sigmund Freud, "Dreams and Occultism," *The Standard Edition of the Complete Psychological Works of Sigmund Freud*, trans. James Strachey [London: Vintage, 1001], 12:39). For Benjamin's interest in telepathy, see, for instance, "Review of the Mendelssohns' *Der Mensch in der Handschrift*" and "Surrealism," in *Selected Writings, Volume* 2, 134, 216.

25. Sigmund Freud, *Civilization and Its Discontents*, trans. James Strachey (New York: Norton, 1961), 92.

26. Walter Benjamin, "Theories of German Fascism: On the Collection of Essays *War and Warriors*, ed. Ernst Jünger," in *Selected Writings, Volume* 2, 312. Benjamin argues, "Any future war will also be a slave revolt on the part of technology" (312).

27. As Ansgar Hillach puts it in his discussion of Benjamin's review when it appeared in English translation for the first time, "Future perspectives are thus narrowed to the heroic 'task' of reconciling the previously disjointed nationalistic powers by means of renewed warfare. Its inevitability is guaranteed as a destiny" (Hillach, "The Aesthetics of Politics: Walter Benjamin's Theories of German Fascism," in *New German Critique* 17 (Spring 1979): 100.

28. Benjamin summarizes the dispute: "There were no witnesses to the events of that night. Of those who were in the train, none was rescued. So to

this very day no one knows what happened—perhaps the storm had blown away the middle of the bridge even before the train arrived, and the train simply plunged into the void. At all events, the storm is said to have raged so furiously that it drowned out all other sounds. But other engineers, especially those who actually built the bridge, maintained that the storm had blown the train off its tracks and hurled it against the parapet" (566–67). Interestingly, then, whatever Benjamin might want to imply by the superiority of knowledge "today," such progress does not necessarily entail recovery or repair of the unknowns of the past. Recent inquiries have not conclusively resolved the issue, though they have called attention to the role of economic interests in the construction of the bridge, a question Benjamin conspicuously avoids. See "We've Still Not Learnt the Lessons of the Tay Bridge Rail Disaster," *Daily Telegraph*, London, August 27, 2006.

29. J. J. Grandville, *Un Autre Monde* (Paris, 1844): 138–39.

30. Benjamin, *Arcades Project*, 8. For further references by Benjamin to Grandville, and to the Saturn image in particular, see *The Arcades Project*, 18–19, 151, 200–201, and 885–87.

31. Ibid., 18. Marx's notion of the "metaphysical subtleties and theological niceties" of the commodity appears at the beginning of "The Fetishism of the Commodity and Its Secret," or part 4 of chapter 1 of *Capital*, vol. 1, trans. Ben Fowkes (London: Penguin, 1976), 163. The subject of Benjamin's relationship to and appropriation of marxism has a long critical bibliography. Speaking specifically of Grandville as a figure in Benjamin's work and of Benjamin's wrong turn toward a marxian rhetoric in *The Arcades Project*, T. J. Clark has argued, "Marxism got in the way of the wonderful poetic-ethnological simplicity of *The Arcades Project* as first conceived in the later 1920s. It muddied, multiplied, and mechanized the project's original outlines; so that finally, essentially, Marxism can only be seen as a cancer on Benjamin's work—on what should have become the last and greatest of surrealist grapplings with the nineteenth century, a settling of accounts with all the mad dreams of Grandpa and Grandville and Victor Hugo" (Clark, "Should Benjamin Have Read Marx?" in *boundary* 2 30, no. 1 [2003]: 32).

32. Walter Benjamin, "The Mississippi Flood, 1927," trans. Jonathan Lutes, in *Walter Benjamin on Radio*, ed. Lecia Rosenthal (Verso, forthcoming). The German, "Die Mississippi-Überschwemmung 1927," appears in Benjamin, *Gesammelte Schriften*, vol. 7.1, pp. 237–43. All subsequent references will appear in the body of the text.

33. See John M. Barry, *Rising Tide: The Great Mississippi Flood of 1927 and How It Changed America* (New York: Simon and Schuster, 1997), esp. 313–43, where Barry discusses the violent conditions under which the refugee camps, most of them atop the remaining levees, became virtual prisons for the hundreds of thousands of African Americans stranded in the "care" of the National Guard, the Red Cross, and local militia. Often at gunpoint, men were

forced into compulsory labor. Barry's account, while useful in its breadth and detail, particularly in its history of the levee system, carries an oddly unacknowledged rhetoric of naturalized "darkness" associated with the river ("There was something dark about the Mississippi, darker even than the rest of the South. And it would grow darker still" [121]). Indeed, not everyone is Conrad.

34. See, for instance, Lothrop Stoddard, *The Rising Tide of Color against White World-Supremacy* (New York: Scribner, 1920). For Stoddard, whiteness is an embankment system which, in the aftermath of the First World War, finds itself apocalyptically breached, opening onto a "general race cataclysm."

35. Emily Apter, " 'Je ne crois pas beaucoup à la literature comparée': Universal Poetics and Postcolonial Comparatism," in *Comparative Literature in an Age of Globalization*, ed. Haun Saussy (Baltimore: Johns Hopkins University Press, 2006): 54–62.

36. Ibid., 60.

37. Ibid., 61.

38. Gayatri Chakravorty Spivak, *Death of a Discipline* (New York: Columbia University Press, 2003), 72.

39. Ibid., 73.

40. Ibid.

4. ON THE LATE SUBLIME: W. G. SEBALD'S *THE RINGS OF SATURN*

1. Available at http://goldenrecord.org/. In addition to the image of the object itself, the site contains the complete archive of the images and sounds stored on the record. For the history of the project, see Carl Sagan et al., *Murmurs of Earth: The Voyager Interstellar Record* (New York: Random House, 1978).

2. The exhibit's collected photographs, and photographs of the exhibit during its launching appearance at New York's Museum of Modern Art, are reproduced with an introduction by Steichen in *The Family of Man* (New York: Simon and Schuster, 1955). Carl Sandburg's prologue demonstrates the exhibition's postwar–cold-war ideology of unity in the spectacle of consuming (self-)representative images. For two critical readings of the widely disseminated, exceptionally popular exhibit, see Roland Barthes, "The Great Family of Man," in *Mythologies*, trans. Annette Lavers (New York: Farrar, Straus and Giroux, 1990), 100–102; and Susan Sontag, *On Photography* (New York: Picador, 1977), 32–33. For Siegfried Kracauer's view of the exhibit's utopianism, see *Theory of Film: The Redemption of Physical Reality* (Princeton: Princeton University Press, 1997), 310.

3. The figure of the alien is a conveniently neutral blank, an always available space for imagining the human (as if) seen by and as an other. The alien

exteriorizes difference, desire, authority, power, knowledge, and above all the future of terrestrial memory, a form of symbolic survival beyond the end of the symbolic. An archive drifting in space, the *Voyager* will represent the human after the last: "Billions of years from now our sun, then a distended red giant star, will have reduced Earth to a charred cinder. But the Voyager record will still be largely intact, in some other remote region of the Milky Way galaxy, preserving a murmur of an ancient civilization" (*Murmurs of Earth*, 42). If the record's economization of the alien-as-other represses the lingering problematic of the other "within," neatly deterritorializing alterity and thereby enabling a homogenization of man-as-species at home and as one, the fantasy of the *Voyager* as archival remainder redoubles the gesture: in the projection of a future shared in cosmic death.

4. The reference to *Voyager II* appears at the close of the novel's fourth chapter (W. G. Sebald, *The Rings of Saturn*, trans. Michael Hulse [New York: New Directions Press, 1998], 99). The image, which I discuss in detail below, appears in the third section, on pages 60–61. All subsequent references to *The Rings of Saturn* will be made parenthetically in the text. For the German, see *Die Ringe des Saturn: Eine Englische Wallfahrt* (Frankfurt am Main: Eichborn Verlag, 1995). It is worth giving brief note to the German subtitle, cryptically held back in the English edition: *An English Pilgrimage*, a phrase about which I have more to say below.

5. Jean-Luc Nancy, "The Sublime Offering," in *Of the Sublime: Presence in Question*, trans. Jeffrey S. Librett (Albany: State University of New York Press, 1993), 27.

6. For a discussion of contemporary theory and the problems raised in conjunction with sublimity and the discourses of the Holocaust, see Dominick LaCapra, *History in Transit* (Ithaca, N.Y.: Cornell University Press, 2004), esp. 144–94. The critical literature related to the twentieth-century sublime, particularly the sublime as it relates to the representation of atrocity, genocide, and terror, is enormous. I will cite selectively rather than attempt to cover the field. Georges Didi-Huberman, in "Images Malgré Tout," in *Mémoire des Camps*, ed. Clément Chéroux (Paris: Éditions Marval, 2001], 219–41), argues forcefully against invoking or remaining invested in the limits of the imagination. Focusing specifically on the representation of Auschwitz found in four photographic images taken secretly from inside the gas chambers at Birkenau, the argument maintains the centrality of the imagination rather than its failure. The achievement of the essay, in my mind, is that the "unimaginable," which we are reminded not to call upon, to summon as justification for ignorance or immanent limit to comprehension ("Donc, n'invoquons pas l'inimaginable," 219), nonetheless persists: Precisely in the face of such evidence, evidence "despite everything" as carried in the existence of the image, the

unimaginable (*that* such photographs should exist) remains—to have been vanquished. For Didi-Huberman's dismissal of Lyotard, see 219n2. See also Georges Didi-Huberman, *Images Malgré Tout* (Paris: Les Éditions de Minuit, 2003), and Georges Didi-Huberman, *Images in Spite of All: Four Photographs from Auschwitz*, trans. Shane B. Lillis (Chicago: University of Chicago Press, 2008).

7. Andreas Huyssen praises Spiegelman's *Maus* because "it marks the limits of mimetic approximation, but it marks them in a pragmatic way and without resorting to sublime new definitions of the sublime as the unpresentable within presentation" (*Present Pasts* [Stanford: Stanford University Press, 2003], 133), a clear-enough critique of Lyotard, though Huyssen does not mention him by name. See also 172n11 for the link to Adorno. Many have attacked Lyotard, but Jacques Rancière has provided the most sustained and convincing discussion of the limits of his argument. See Jacques Rancière, *The Future of the Image*, trans. Gregory Elliott (London: Verso, 2007), esp. 130–38. For a discussion of the debates surrounding the contemporary sublime, particularly the sublime in relationship to "human-inflicted disaster," see Gene Ray, "Reading the Lisbon Earthquake: Adorno, Lyotard, and the Contemporary Sublime," in *Terror and the Sublime in Art and Critical Theory: From Auschwitz to Hiroshima to September 11* (New York: Palgrave, 2005).

8. Jean-François Lyotard, "What Is Postmodernism?" in *The Postmodern Condition: A Report on Knowledge*, trans. Geoff Bennington and Brian Massumi (Minneapolis: University of Minnesota Press, 1984), 81.

9. The citation to Kant is from *Critique of Judgment*, trans. Werner S. Pluhar (Indianapolis: Hackett, 1987), 105. It is worth restating that for Kant the sublime is not an issue of the object but rather of the subject's experience of itself and its (superior) faculties in relation to the object. In this case, regarding the failure of the imagination in regard to reason's demand for "absolute totality as a real idea," Kant concludes, "*Sublime is what even to be able to think proves that the mind has a power surpassing any standard of sense*" (106).

10. Edmund Burke, *A Philosophical Enquiry into the Origin of Our Ideas of the Sublime and the Beautiful* (Oxford: Oxford University Press, 1990), 59–60. The citation is from the subsection on "Power," where Burke links sublimity and terror ("terror, the common stock of every thing that is sublime").

11. It is in this context that Baudrillard's questionable argument of the "manufactured catastrophe" becomes, in its own right, far too cute; Baudrillard is hardly saying much when he hyperbolically links our desire to "enjoy the show" to our "hastening [of] the end of the world by all possible means," a link that he argues points to a kind of fear of apocalypse-deprivation (see Jean Baudrillard, *Cool Memories*, trans. Chris Turner [London: Verso, 1990], 229). This argument simply spins the familiar notion of an anaesthetized

bourgeois culture into a late form of hysterical decadence, a madness of ener-
vation that produces its symptoms in the production of the "artificial catastrophe" (Jean Baudrillard, *The Illusion of the End*, trans. Chris Turner [Stanford:
Stanford University Press, 1994], 71). More problematic is Baudrillard's cynical refusal to differentiate between the historical manufacturing of catastrophe, which certainly has been known to come with its perversions and
pleasures, and the aspecific "collective desire for catastrophe," which is "also
a playing at catastrophe" (see Jean Baudrillard, *America*, trans. Chris Turner
[London: Verso, 1994], 42).

   12. Virginia Woolf, "How It Strikes a Contemporary," in *The Common
Reader* (San Diego: Harvest, 1984), 231–41.

   13. Hans Magnus Enzensberger, "A Theory of Tourism," *New German
Critique*, no. 68 (1996): 117–35.

   14. Žižek's discussion of the sublime, unlike that of many others today,
does not orbit around questions of representation and the Holocaust. Žižek
argues that at work within the leveling effects of commodity culture, the sublime and its elevations become an issue of the preservation, through art itself,
of the "minimal gap" that signifies a difference between the "(Sacred) Place"
and the Void of the Place, or the entry into the symbolic and psychosis. See
Slavoj Žižek, *The Fragile Absolute* (London: Verso, 2000), 32–50.

   15. For a bibliography of Sebald, including his critical works prior to the
publication of *Nach der Natur: Ein Elementargedicht* in 1988, see *Searching for
Sebald: Photography after Sebald*, ed. Lise Patt (Los Angeles: Institute of Cultural Inquiry, 2007), 606–8. For an excellent discussion of the "timeliness" of
Sebald's work and of the failure of criticism to address its own "conservative
pleasure" in its desire to desire his texts, see Stewart Martin, "W. G. Sebald
and the Modern Art of Memory," *Radical Philosophy* 132 (July/August 2005):
18–30.

   16. One might speculate that Sebald's hybrid forms have provided, among
their many other productive effects, criticism with an occasion—as if under
the cover of alibi, an excuse that claims not to need one—to reinvest in issues
of form. Received with an ampleness of welcome, Sebald presents, it would
seem, a long-awaited invitation, an offering of an aesthetics that rewards by
disclaiming (and for some, perhaps going so far as to heal) the divisions that
would separate the interests of form ("formalism" is the term of abuse) from
those of historicism (diffused into the broad formation of "cultural studies,"
the charges for and against historicism are, perhaps, less identifiable these
days). In reconsidering the significance of form, the obvious point of reference
is Adorno. Stewart Martin, who notes that there "is a sense of fulfilled anticipation in the reception of Sebald's art, even *gratitude*" ("W. G. Sebald and the
Modern Art of Memory," 19; emphasis added), turns to Adorno for a critical
reading of the historical, dialectical significance of form (27–29). Though

Martin is hardly unique in wanting to address Sebald's history of reception, to my mind his critical treatment of the object, that is to say in his approach to framing and analyzing the Sebaldian moment, is rare in problematizing (which is not to say avoiding) the seductive enticements of transferential desire. (Is not "gratitude" one word for the sustained expectations—for truth, for infinite understanding, for deliverance, at last, from the perils of misrecognition—at work in transference?) For a discussion of transference in the context of Holocaust criticism, see Dominick LaCapra, "Representing the Holocaust: Reflections on the Historians' Debate," in *Probing the Limits of Representation: Nazism and the "Final Solution,"* ed. Saul Friedlander (Cambridge: Harvard University Press, 1992), 108–27; see also LaCapra's *Representing the Holocaust: History, Theory, Trauma* (Ithaca, N.Y.: Cornell University Press, 1994), which includes a slightly amended version of the essay and extends his discussion of the psychoanalytic vocabulary in relation to reading the past and an ethics of historiographic practice. In *History and Memory after Auschwitz* (Ithaca, N.Y.: Cornell University Press, 1998) and in *History in Transit: Experience, Identity, Critical Theory* (Ithaca, N.Y.: Cornell University Press, 2004), LaCapra increasingly emphasizes the categories of "acting-out" and "working-through," with particular investment in the work of the latter. For an extended discussion of these categories alongside that of transference, see *History in Transit*, chap. 2. One of the difficulties of LaCapra's deployment of transference emerges in the shifting relay of "positions": If the initial analogy casts the historian as analyst, and by extension the object of study as analysand, it morphs into a model in which the object of study is the historian, or the historian as studied by herself, even and especially if "by herself" she is already in relationship to an other. Thus, "by transference, I mean primarily one's implication in the other or the object of study with the tendency to repeat in one's own discourse or practice tendencies active in, or projected into, the other or object" (*History in Transit*, 74). Another difficulty, on view here, is the definition of transference as acting out, an iterative extension of the tendency to repeat, which LaCapra opposes to empathy, and, more generally, to a process of working-through that is social, dialogic, open not only to an ideational alterity but to the voice of an empirical other. For literary criticism, the difficulty becomes, or continues to be, locating and claiming such alterity, in and as the voice of the text.

17. Woolf, "How It Strikes a Contemporary," 236.

18. For Blanchot's comments on Woolf and the ambivalent catastrophe that falls upon a work's completion (Woolf calls the effect a "sinking down"), see Maurice Blanchot, "The Failure of the Demon: The Vocation," in *The Book to Come*, trans. Charlotte Mandell (Stanford: Stanford University Press, 2003), 97–104. It is in this essay that Woolf's work gives Blanchot to ask, "Is

there a way to gather together what is dispersed, to make continuous the discontinuous and to maintain the wandering in a nonetheless unified whole?" (101), a question whose significant tension remains relevant to my discussion above. That is, how to think the relationship between the untethered allowance of wandering, or the undecided itinerary without which the work cannot begin, and the persistent threat of the in-completion of the work? For an extended, more explicitly nonpsychological discussion of the dialectic of the "void" written through the book, see Blanchot's "The Absence of the Book," in *The Infinite Conversation*, trans. Susan Hanson (Minneapolis: University of Minnesota Press, 1993).

19. *Oxford English Dictionary.*

20. The letter can be found, with facing English translation, in *The Collected Letters of Joseph Conrad*, vol. 1, ed. Frederick R. Karl and Laurence Davies (Cambridge: Cambridge University Press, 1990), 42–44. The translation reads, "Above all, we must forgive the unhappy souls who have elected to make the pilgrimage on foot, who skirt the shore and look uncomprehendingly upon the horror of the struggle, the joy of victory, the profound hopelessness of the vanquished" (43). When in the letter, Conrad, who is writing "on the theme of forgiveness," implores his aunt to forgive, the offending party, one of the "unhappy souls," remains unnamed. From the context, the implication is that Conrad hopes that his aunt will grant forgiveness (invoked as an ideal in the pursuit of "Divine Justice . . . which is the only hope, the only refuge of souls who have fought, suffered, and succumbed in the struggle with life" [43]) to her late husband, as well as to herself and those around her, and finally to Conrad himself. Interestingly, Conrad's agile prose suggests that the "unhappy souls," those who "skirt the shore" and remain as if apart, mere "uncomprehending" onlookers to the struggle, are to be understood as doing so out of torment, an excess of suffering that makes them all the more blind to their part in a general economy of horror, the "horror of the struggle."

21. Dehiscence is the split in opening that gives, in the double act of gaping open, more space or room for another. I am thinking of Derrida's spin on the term: "This word marks emphatically that the divided opening, in the growth of a plant, is also what, in a *positive* sense, makes production, reproduction, development possible. Dehiscence (like iterability) limits what it makes possible, while rendering its rigor and purity impossible. What I at work here is something like a law of undecidable contamination" (Jacques Derrida, *Limited Inc*, trans. Samuel Weber [Evanston, Ill.: Northwestern University Press, 1988], 59).

22. Jacques Rancière, *The Future of the Image*, trans. Gregory Elliott (London: Verso, 2007), 120.

23. The strange: I think one can read the category as a nontechnical, almost prosaic (if such an assimilation were not paradoxical to the term itself) phrasing of the "uncanny" and precisely in the way the latter problematizes

the distinction between the familiar-possible and the unfamiliar-impossible, so Woolf's interest in Browne hovers in the unresolved tension. For Woolf, Browne, unlike so many of her contemporaries, writes "of human fate and death, of the immensity of the past, of the strangeness which surrounds us on every side" ("Sir Thomas Browne," in *The Essays of Virginia Woolf*, vol. 3, ed. Andrew McNeillie [San Diego: Harcourt, 1988], 369). The "strange," then, an attentiveness to a lack of reality within reality, or as Woolf writes, Browne's "power of bringing the remote and incongruous astonishingly together . . . the most exquisite sense of mysterious affinities between ghosts and roses" (370). Elsewhere, Woolf delights in the incongruity between a physician's mastery and the writer's play. "The strangest ideas and emotions have play in him, as he goes about his work, outwardly the most sober of mankind, and esteemed the greatest physician in Norwich" (Woolf, "Reading," in *The Essays*, 3:155).

24. Here it is worthwhile to recall that Woolf, even in her literary criticism, is not interested in building a system or battling over established terminologies (whether from literary criticism, philosophy, psychoanalysis, religion, or any other field). Hence, the "strange" as it appears in her essays, though it intersects with the conceptual terrain of the uncanny, not to mention those of the gothic, the fantastic, and Brecht's *V-Effekte*, is precisely not "elevated" to the status of a concept or a theory. And hasn't this always been part of the trouble with the uncanny? To the extent that we want it to remain available to signify an unsettled and unsettling effect—in language, perception, affect, art—we must yield to a certain, yet precisely uncertain, allowance for the term's unwieldy mobility. And if such uncertain allowance for uncertainty brings with it anticipation of the charge of useless obfuscation, unwarranted difficulty, or excessive lack of clarity, we might be justified, if overly optimistic, in hoping that Woolf's essay, "Reading," might be of some assistance. Here Woolf addresses, apropos Sir Thomas Browne's texts, the likelihood that they would incur an "obstinate resistance" in her contemporaries, a resistance to "difficulty" ("Reading," 158–59) for which Woolf offers an explanation well worth reading. See Woolf, "Reading," 153–59.

25. Theodor Adorno, "Parataxis," in *Notes to Literature*, vol. 2, ed. Rolf Tiedemann, trans. Shierry Weber Nicholsen (New York: Columbia University Press, 1992), 131. One could connect Adorno's reading of Hölderlin's dialectical metaphysics to the function of nature and natural history in Sebald, particularly as they appear in Sebald's return to the notion of a "natural history of destruction." Andreas Huyssen has criticized Sebald for maintaining the ahistorical, metaphysical zone of the natural; Huyssen argues that through such a retreat into nature (particularly in the essays of *On the Natural History of Destruction*, trans. Anthea Bell [New York: Modern Library, 2004]), Sebald

repeats, in the manner of what Huyssen calls a blind spot, the apocalyptic fantasy of a pure break with the past, a desire for the radically new that is, for obvious reasons, historically compromised within the context of postwar German culture. See Huyssen, *Present Pasts*, 150, 157. Alternatively, Adorno's reading of Hölderlin's late hymns, which admittedly is more complex that I can do justice to here, finds in them, and in particular in their form, an "aconceptual synthesis," which, like music, allows for the determinate negation of the subject's domination of nature. I have wondered if it might be possible to read Sebald's fascination with the appearance of nature in forms of decay, dispersal, and self-destruction (coastal erosion and storms, for instance) not as refusals to acknowledge the force and inescapable effects of history or as alibis for or analogues to the history of (in)human destruction but rather as a way of interrupting (negative?) fantasies of human mastery as all and absolute. Such would be the utopian, perhaps mythic, gesture in Sebald, the attempt to cede to and affirm alterity without recoding the chaotic, unreconciled nonmeaning in an already completed and exhausted synthesis. "Genius, which cancels the cycle of domination and nature, is not wholly unlike nature; it has that affinity with it without which, as Plato knew, experience of the Other is not possible" (Adorno, "Parataxis," 148).

26. Walter Benjamin, *The Arcades Project*, trans. Howard Eiland and Kevin McLaughlin (Cambridge: Harvard University Press, 1999), 211.

27. Sebald, *Die Ringe des Saturn*, 79.

28. Barthes's exposition of the neutral is precisely *not* a matter of indifference or lack of intensity. "I define the Neutral as that which outplays [*déjoue*] the paradigm, or rather I call Neutral everything that baffles the paradigm. . . . My definition of the Neutral remains structural. By which I mean that, for me, the Neutral doesn't refer to 'impressions' of grayness, of 'neutrality,' of indifference. The Neutral—my Neutral—can refer to intense, strong, unprecedented states. 'To outplay the paradigm' is an ardent, burning activity" (Roland Barthes, *The Neutral*, trans. Rosalind E. Krauss and Denis Hollier (New York: Columbia University Press, 2005), 6–7.

29. Mark Anderson reads the uncertain documentary status of the image in Sebald and Kluge, arguing that both authors, "in classic modernist fashion," challenge "the reader to believe in and simultaneously doubt the authenticity of their images," a challenge that serves to "ultimately question the notion that the world and its representations can be divided into entirely separate categories of truth and fiction, into factual 'documents' and aesthetic constructs. There is no 'pure' historical document" (Mark Anderson, "Documents, Photography, Postmemory: Alexander Kluge, W. G. Sebald, and the German Family," *Poetics Today* 29, no. 1 [2008]: 150). So far, it would be difficult to disagree with Anderson's assessment. More complicated, however, is

Anderson's historicist-ethical take on Sebald's aesthetics of epistemological shake-up. Against the historically normative (if also distinctly troubled) postwar impassivity and alienation endorsed by Kluge's texts, Sebald, according to Anderson, writes "empathic narratives," or stories of suffering through which the narrator (who, for Anderson, is Sebald, and at the same time a representative figure of the "second generation," defined as those who live "without any direct experience of this war") attempts to "bridge the gap and connect himself imaginatively to its [the war's] participants" (151). Anderson dubs this forging of connection an aesthetics of "familiarization," the articulation of a longing to "'familiarize' and personalize" the experience of the past. Such appropriative identification, for Anderson, represents a politically necessary rupture with a postwar refusal of familiarity, or the abjection of war experience in a postwar culture that promoted and survived on gestures of disidentification and dissociation. The refusal of a refusal, then, Sebald's aesthetics would offer something of an affirmative synthesis, an antinumbing evocation of pain. As I suggested in my discussion of Woolf and the prose of strangeness, the difficulty here is in sustaining the tension between the cold aesthetics of disinheritance and the becalmed warmth implied by the notion of familiarity. Anderson, who notes a "focus on family relations" in Sebald's *Austerlitz* and *The Emigrants* (141), tends to agree with the readings of J. J. Long and Marianne Hirsch, concluding that Sebald's prose of "postmemory" effects a compensatory, restorative, inclusive space of belonging (141, 151). "Melancholic but also strangely restorative, these ghostlike pictures attempt nothing less than to bring the dead to life—even as they question the reality of the living" (151). It is just such a fantasy of restoration and reanimation that I want to question. See also Anderson's earlier work on Sebald, "The Edge of Darkness: On W. G. Sebald" (*October* 106 [Fall 2003]: 102–21), which is far less resolved on a redemptive reading.

   30. The narrator wants to argue that the painting is organized around a dissimulated void in the place of vision's object, such that, "it is debatable whether anyone ever really saw that body, since the art of anatomy, then in its infancy, was not least a way of making the reprobate body invisible" (13). The painter calls attention to the uncertain place of the dead body, the narrator suggests, by having the physicians look instead at an "open anatomical atlas" (13). In the second reproduction of the painting, the atlas is cut off, no longer in our view. The narrator's voice, then, has all the more authority to read and explain the painting's central contradiction and meaning for us, and to do so as if with and in the mind of the painter, whose "deliberate intent" he sees and understands. Through a "crass misrepresentation at the exact centre point of its meaning" (16), in other words the dissection of a hand that is painted "anatomically the wrong way round," the painter succeeds not only in exposing the blind spot of the physicians but also in making heard his own intention

and its meaning: "He alone sees that greenish annihilated body [of the dead man, Aris Kindt], and he alone sees the shadow in the half-open mouth and over the dead man's eyes" (17).

31. Adrian Daub, "'Donner à Voir': The Logics of the Caption in W. G. Sebald's *Rings of Saturn* and Alexander Kluge's *Devil's Blind Spot*," in *Searching for Sebald: Photography after Sebald*, ed. Lise Patt (Los Angeles: Institute of Cultural Inquiry, 2007), 324. Despite what appears to be a fanciful desire to read all images as if "after" Sebald (and, barring any uniform understanding of what that would mean, perhaps to read Sebald "after" Boltanski), I agree with some of the arguments made in Daub's essay.

32. Walter Benjamin, "The Storyteller," in *Illuminations*, trans. Harry Zohn (New York: Schocken, 1968), 84. For the dating of the backlog, see Ben Shephard, *After Daybreak: The Liberation of Bergen-Belsen, 1945* (New York: Schocken, 2005), 75; also see Jon Bridgman, *The End of the Holocaust: The Liberation of the Camps* (London: B. T. Batsford, 1990), 53ff., on the burial of the more than 10,000 unburied corpses the British found on their arrival, along with the 13,000 who died after April 15; for a starkly worded timeline, see *The Relief of Belsen: April 1945, Eye Witness Accounts* (London: Imperial War Museum, 1991), 7, from which, a few excerpts, which I cite for their echoes: 18 April, "The burial of the dead. At first the SS guards are made to collect the bodies and bury them. Eventually a bulldozer has to be used . . ."; 28 April, "The burial of the dead is complete" (7).

33. The quotation interpolates Browne's phrasing into Sebald's without distinction. "The iniquity of oblivion blindly scatters her poppyseed" is the only distinct phrase taken from Browne, *Hydrotaphia, Urne-Buriall, or A Discourse of the Sepulchrall Urnes Lately Found in Norfolk* [1658], chap. 5, online at http://penelope.uchicago.edu/hgc.html.

34. Clément Chéroux, 'L'épiphanie négative: production, diffusion et réception des photographie de la libération des camps," in *Mémoire des Camps*, 126–27. Chéroux includes two photographs taken by Rodger in the development of this argument.

35. George Rodger's work and life have been widely documented, particularly in the context of the history of the Magnum photo agency, which, along with Henri Cartier-Bresson, Robert Capa, and David Seymour, he cofounded in 1947. During the Second World War, Rodger worked for *Life* as a photographer, and it was in this context that he photographed Bergen-Belsen, where he arrived shortly after the camp was liberated by the British. The official date of liberation is typically given as April 15, 1945. (Sebald gives the date as the 14th.) As recounted by his biographer, Carole Naggar, who had access to Rodger's unpublished wartime diaries, Rodger arrived at Belsen on April 20 (Carole Naggar, *George Rodger: An Adventure in Photography, 1908–1995* [Syracuse:

Syracuse University Press, 2003], 136). This dating is significant because, as it is so often said that Rodger was the "first photographer to enter the concentration camp at Bergen-Belsen" (Jinx Rodger, *Guardian*, March 15, 2008; Jinx Rodger was George Rodger's second wife), one might easily fail to take note of the fact that the photographs he took were of the camp five days into the liberation. The photograph by Rodger reprinted in *The Rings of Saturn* can be found in George Rodger, *Humanity and Inhumanity: The Photographic Journey of George Rodger* (London: Phaidon Press, 1994), 135; and in Clément Chéroux, ed., *Mémoire des Camps: Photographies des Camps de Concentration et d'Extermination Nazis, 1933–1999* (Paris: Éditions Marval, 2001), 141. As for Rodger's relative obscurity, as the *New York Times* put it in his obituary, "Long overshadowed by . . . Robert Capa and Henri Cartier-Bresson, Mr. Roger [*sic*] was best known for photographs he took at the Bergen-Belsen concentration camp when it was liberated by British troops in April 1945" (July 26, 1995).

36. Roland Barthes, *Camera Lucida: Reflections on Photography*, trans. Richard Howard (New York: Hill and Wang, 1981), 77. For a brief, incredibly useful overview of the indexical as it emerges in critical discussions of photography, in particular in Rosalind Krauss's work on Pierce, see Mary Ann Doane, "Indexicality: Trace and Sign: Introduction," *differences* 18, no. 1 (2007): 1–6.

37. David Campany has argued that the function of the "late photograph" is to stabilize the slide of information in a culture of density and overload. See "Safety in Numbness: Some Remarks on Problems of 'Late Photography,'" in *The Cinematic*, ed. David Campany (Cambridge: MIT Press, 2007). See also Vicki Goldberg on the photographic "icon" that seems "to provide an instant and effortless connection to some deeply meaningful moment in history. They seem to summarize such complex phenomena as the powers of the human spirit or of universal destruction" (Vicki Goldberg, *The Power of Photography: How Photographs Changed Our Lives* [New York: Abbeville Press, 1991], 135). Such arguments seem largely to echo, without the critical resonances, the observations made by Christian Metz in "Photography and Fetish," *October* 34 (Autumn 1985): 81–90.

38. Daub, "'Donner à Voir,'" 318.

39. Daub, largely indebted to the work of Ulrich Baer, wants to argue that with this image, "Sebald is in dialogue with certain traditions of landscape depiction. . . . Rather than opening up before our eyes, this landscape is closed to us, offering no place in which the subject can 'find' itself within the picture frame" (322). For Baer's essay on landscape photography and the troubled "place" of Holocaust memory, see "To Give Memory a Place: Contemporary Holocaust Photography and the Landscape Tradition," in his *Spectral Evidenc: The Photography of Trauma* (Cambridge: MIT Press, 2005).

40. Bourke-White's widely reproduced image ("Survivors behind Barbed Wire, Buchenwald 1945") was taken in April 1945 for *Life*. Unlike other photographs she took at the camp, some of which were far more graphic in their representations of mass death, the image was not published at the time. One can speculate that despite the image's becoming an icon, it was not immediately published in *Life* (which would reproduce it later for purposes of commemoration) precisely because it is less vigorously aimed at death; rather than corpses, skeletal remains, or humans so nearly at the point of death they cannot return the camera's gaze, the image is of men standing, many of whom look directly at the camera. For a discussion of this image and its history, see Barbie Zelizer, *Remembering to Forget: Holocaust Memory through the Camera's Eye* (Chicago: University of Chicago Press, 1998), 181–85. Discussing the image's iterative canonization, Zelizer reads the fact that *Life* recycled it as part of its effort to "systematically connect the atrocities with photography" (166), an argument she extends to include the somewhat less (or perhaps just differently) systematic, yet entirely common (and, in a Derridean sense, inevitable—from the start) practice of reproducing the same image in changing contexts, such that "photographs were used to represent a wide range of events, not all of them directly related to what was being depicted, such as when *Time* used a picture of Belsen victims to illustrate an article commemorating V-E Day" (180). For more on Bourke-White, see *Mémoire des Camps*, 134–39. Marianne Hirsch discusses the image as it appears, redrawn, in the original version of Art Spiegelman's *Maus*, in Marianne Hirsch, "Surviving Images: Holocaust Photographs and the Work of Postmemory," in *Visual Culture and the Holocaust*, ed. Barbie Zelizer (New Brunswick, N.J.: Rutgers University Press, 2001). Finally, for Mucha's photograph, taken between mid-February and mid-March 1945, see *Mémoire des Camps*, 102.

41. See Zelizer, *Remembering to Forget*, and Joanne Reilly, *Belsen: The Liberation of a Camp* (London: Routledge, 1998).

42. See Georges Didi-Huberman, *Images in Spite of All: Four Photographs from Auschwitz*, trans. Shane B. Lillis (Chicago: University of Chicago Press, 2008).

43. Hirsch, "Surviving Images," 238.

44. Ibid.; emphasis added. The emphasis on the possibility of regaining a position—here the improved position of regaining a "capacity to enable a postmemorial working through"—posits a mixed goal and ideal held in place under the notion of "working through." Rhetorically, the place of this ideal is divided between a future cast as the "new" (as suggested by the narrative in which iconic images are situated in "new texts and new contexts") and a gainful outcome that would restore to the individual or collective subject an already achieved, already understood, and well grasped (at least in concept) position of ability.

45. Eduardo Cadava, "*Lapsus Imaginis*: The Image in Ruins," *October* 96 (Spring 2001): 49.

46. Moses Mendelssohn, *Philosophical Writings*, ed. and trans. Daniel O. Dahlstrom (Cambridge: Cambridge University Press, 1997), 202.

47. Ibid., 200.

48. Here I disagree with Zachary Braiterman's critique of the sublime in Holocaust discourse. Braiterman, relying on Schiller, puts forward the importance of the naive *over* the sublime. "Against Holocaust-Sublime: Naive Reference and the Generation of Memory," *History and Memory* 12, no. 2 (2001): 7–28.

TOWARD A CONCLUSION: THE IN-EXHAUSTIBLE CATASTROPHE

1. For the relationship between theory and the problem of an exhaustion of resources—including the rhetorical-political resource of the claims of resistance, difference, and antisystematic or (anti-)Hegelian thought, see Mark C. Taylor, *The Moment of Complexity* (Chicago: University of Chicago Press, 2001). Taylor's take on the institutionalization of the marginal ("As the marginal becomes institutionally central, the theoretical concern with difference and otherness is gradually transformed into a preoccupation with the same," 48) proposes a more nuanced—one might say rehabilitated—understanding of the complexities at work in Hegel, an argument that finds interesting echoes in Derrida's critique of an insistence on the "non-dialecticizable" (see, for instance, Jacques Derrida, *A Taste for the Secret*, trans. Giacomo Donis [Cambridge: Polity, 2001], 32–34).

2. Gilles Deleuze, "The Exhausted," in *Essays Critical and Clinical*, trans. Daniel W. Smith and Michael A. Greco (Minneapolis: University of Minnesota Press, 1997), 152–74.

3. Virginia Woolf, "Mr. Bennett and Mrs. Brown," in *The Captain's Death Bed and Other Essays* (San Diego: Harvest, 1950), 117.

4. Jean-François Lyotard, "The Sublime and the Avant-Garde," in *The Inhuman*, trans. Geoffrey Bennington and Rachel Bowlby (Stanford: Stanford University Press, 1991), 91; see also *The Differend: Phrases in Dispute*, trans. Georges Van Den Abbeele (Minneapolis: University of Minnesota Press, 1988), 80.

5. Theodor Adorno, *Aesthetic Theory*, trans. Robert Hullot-Kentor (Minneapolis: University of Minnesota Press, 1997), 22.

6. Virginia Woolf, "Modern Fiction," in *The Common Reader* (San Diego: Harvest, 1984), 150.

7. Deleuze, "The Exhausted," 152.

8. Ibid., 152, 154.

9. Ibid., 156–57.

10. Alain Finkielkraut, *The Imaginary Jew*, trans. Kevin O'Neill and David Suchoff (Lincoln: University of Nebraska Press, 1994), 82, 15. Karl Marx, *The Eighteenth Brumaire of Louis Bonaparte*, in *Surveys from Exile* (New York: Penguin, 1973).

INDEX